The Hottest Seat on Campus

The Hottest Seat on Campus

A Roadmap for Mastering Leadership in College Admission

ANGEL B. PÉREZ

HARVARD EDUCATION PRESS
CAMBRIDGE, MASSACHUSETTS

Paperback ISBN 9798895570210
Library of Congress Cataloging-in-Publication Data is on file.

Published by Harvard Education Press,
an imprint of the Harvard Education Publishing Group

Harvard Education Press
8 Story Street
Cambridge, MA 02138

Cover Design: Eric Wilder
Cover Image: New Africa via Shutterstock

The typefaces in this book are Adobe Garamond Pro and Myriad Pro.

This book is dedicated to all of my admission and counseling colleagues worldwide who tirelessly strive to enhance the lives of their students and institutions.

You are my inspiration.

Contents

Foreword

Who are the next generation of admission deans?" I asked my colleague. I vividly remember this conversation from more than ten years ago. We had been discussing the push and pull of our respective roles as deans of admission and financial aid: the complexity of developing and executing a successful enrollment strategy; the joys of meeting students where they are, matching promise with possibility and the art and science of "crafting a class"; and the increasing tensions between meeting internal expectations and managing external demographic shifts. Part wistful reflection, part mournful lament, we were genuinely concerned about who the next generation of enrollment leaders would be and how they might be prepared for the evolving landscape.

Leadership in college admission is not for the faint of heart. It demands a balance of strategy and empathy, adaptability, and decisiveness. This calling intertwines institutional priorities with personal passion, professional growth, and the ability to inspire a team toward shared goals.

It is a calling—and a concern—I share with Angel Pérez. Though Angel and I knew of each other through our respective careers in admission, we had never actually met until I had the opportunity to engage with Angel as he began his role as CEO of the National Association for College Admission Counseling (NACAC), a membership organization in which emerging leaders in the profession often find their footing. During our work together and many conversations, Angel and I explored the intricacies of leadership in higher education, exchanging stories of challenges, triumphs, and lessons learned. These dialogues often returned to a central question: *Who will step into these roles in the future, and what will it take for them to thrive?*

This question has guided much of my professional life. Over three decades in college admission, including thirteen years as a dean, I witnessed firsthand the evolving demands of the field. As an admission dean, I navigated the joys and pressures of shaping enrollment strategies, fostering relationships across campus, and guiding teams toward ambitious goals. It was a journey filled with purpose but not without its challenges, many of which have only intensified over time.

When I took the opportunity to transition from an institutional leadership role to a consultant role with an executive search firm, I gained a broader perspective on leadership in higher education. This shift gave me a new lens through which to view the admission profession, allowing me to assess the qualities institutions sought in their leaders and provide advice. From that perspective, I observed a growing complexity in the roles tied to enrollment management, driven by competing priorities, constrained resources, and heightened expectations. The leaders who thrived were not just experts in their functional areas; they were strategic thinkers and skilled communicators, adept at navigating institutional systems.

My current work as an organizational and leadership development consultant deepens this perspective. Organizations are inherently complex systems, often fraught with dysfunction, and navigating them requires exceptional leadership. In my practice, I focus on helping individuals align their passion with purpose and performance while cultivating the self-awareness and adaptability required to thrive in dynamic environments. These principles are vital for today's college admission leaders, who must engage multiple stakeholders and address complex institutional needs with clarity and confidence.

It is from this broad vantage point—practitioner, advisor, and coach—that I see the urgent need for this book. Angel's work comes at a pivotal time for the profession. Today's chief enrollment officers and admission deans occupy what journalist Eric Hoover aptly calls "the hottest seats on campus."[1] The stakes are high. These professionals are often asked to provide simple and swift solutions to complex problems. They are tasked with navigating relationships across campus, leveraging data and emerging technologies, and meeting the increasing pressures of market realities, financial constraints, and competing priorities. The challenge is clear: How do we prepare the next generation of leaders to step into these roles with confidence, competence, and the ability to adapt?

This book is both a guide and a call to action. It asks readers to look beyond the functional aspects of leadership—budget management, recruitment strategies, and enrollment goals—and consider the deeper qualities and characteristics that inspire enduring success. Self-awareness, reflection, and the ability to ask the right questions before offering solutions are emphasized throughout. *How will we show up* in the role and engage with the work? What do we need to *know and under-*

stand about what our key stakeholders—trustees, presidents, faculty and staff colleagues, students, and families—know and understand? Where is there alignment? What are the obstacles to success? These traits are not innate but are developed through intentional practice and continuous learning.

The lessons in this book are deeply relevant for aspiring leaders. Angel's current role affords a clear view of the challenges and opportunities facing admission leaders and the opportunity to share observations grounded in the distinctive mission and purpose of NACAC: to *empower college admission counseling professionals through education, advocacy, and community*. He incorporates years of experience in admission leadership navigating this complex landscape to offer a framework that blends operational expertise with strategic vision. He does not shy away from the challenges inherent in the role but instead uses them as opportunities for growth and learning. His candid reflections, paired with actionable advice, create a space for readers to engage with their own leadership journeys.

Through his own experiences and those offered by other respected admission leaders, Angel emphasizes aligning passion with purpose, cultivating vulnerability as a strength, and fostering an environment of continuous improvement. He highlights the ability to balance inquiry with advocacy, to temper passion with pragmatism, and to understand both one's strengths and one's blind spots as hallmarks of effective leadership.

As someone who has had the benefit of mentorship and the privilege of mentoring others, I can attest to the importance of Angel's approach. This book is a reflection of his commitment to guiding others, much as he has guided his teams and countless others in the profession. It is a primer for those who wish to lead with both head and heart, to align their values with the institutions they serve, and to inspire their teams toward meaningful goals.

Angel writes with a clear purpose: to prepare readers not just to do the work of college admission but to define how we engage it. He asks us to reflect on our own journeys, to take stock of what we bring to the table to inform and influence, and to approach leadership with intention and integrity. In chapter 6, Angel notes, "Becoming a dean of admission can lead to immense joy, meaning, and purpose, but if you don't approach the job strategically by learning to manage yourself, it can lead to burnout and even resentment." This is a powerful reminder of what is at stake. Leadership in enrollment management is as much about understanding oneself as it is about understanding one's institution.

For many of us who dedicated careers to this profession, leadership is a journey of growth. It involves integrating our authentic personal and professional selves to not only prepare for the complexities of the role but also remind us of the joy and purpose that drew us to this work in the first place. For us, "the hottest seat on campus" can also be the best seat in the house, with a view of the many moving parts supporting both institutional and student success and a central role in achieving that.

This book is an invaluable companion for anyone embarking on that path. In these pages, you will find a wealth of insights, strategies, and practical advice. You will be encouraged to reflect on your own experiences and prepare for the challenges ahead. Most important, you will discover how to bring your strengths to the forefront and motivate others to do the same.

So read on. Embrace the opportunity to learn, reflect, and grow. So read on. Take this opportunity to expand your learning, deepen your perspective, and continue your professional growth. The field needs experienced leaders who will step forward with clarity, courage, and conviction. This book will help you strengthen your impact.

Jennifer Desjarlais
Principal, Cambridge Hill Partners
Former Dean of Admission and Financial Aid, Wellesley College

Introduction

Being an admission counselor at a college or university is one of the most joyful and rewarding jobs in the field of education. I know, because a few days after my college graduation, at the ripe old age of twenty-two, I became an admission counselor at my alma mater. When I accepted the job, I decided I would do it for a year, maybe two, or at least until I could find a "real job."

What I didn't realize then is that I would fall in love with the work and the incredible community of people who dedicate their lives to the profession of college admission counseling. I learned there's something very special about a community made up of thousands of people around the globe who, every day, fight for college access. In my experience, most people who do this work joined the profession because they love students, they love the institutions they represent, and they want to see both thrive. They believe in the transformative power of higher education and want to see as many students as possible attain it. Often, their own college experience was life changing, and they want to pay it forward.

This certainly was the case for me. A high school counselor and an admission officer fundamentally changed my life. I attended a public high school in New York City, where most counselors had at least five hundred students in their caseload. Most of the students were from low-income backgrounds and were first-generation high school students. It was a difficult time in New York City. Gang violence and drugs were prevalent in schools, resources were limited, and overcrowded schools were the norm. Most students who attended these public schools didn't grow up knowing about college. I was fortunate, however. In my junior year, a high school counselor took time out of her busy schedule and asked me if

I ever considered going to college. When she asked, I was stunned. The only people I knew who went to college were on television, and I wasn't sure how that could happen for me.

That powerful question alone put my life on an entirely different trajectory. It was what sociologist Roberta Espinoza of Loyola Marymount University calls a "pivotal moment." In her book of the same name, Espinoza posits that every young person needs someone in their life who taps them on the shoulder and shows them what possibilities could lie ahead for them.[1] I was grateful for that first pivotal moment, and for the second—an admission officer visited my high school and painted a picture of what life could be on a college campus. This made me fall in love with the idea of college. I was in awe of that counselor—their ability to tell stories, to inspire young people, and to make dreams come true. Who wouldn't want THAT job?

So, when I graduated from college and was offered a job as an admission counselor at my alma mater, Skidmore College, I couldn't believe my luck. Having grown up in a low-income background in the projects of the South Bronx, I never imagined I could go to college, much less work at one. As a young admission counselor, I traveled all over the country to recruit students to a school I loved. From Omaha to Des Moines, Los Angeles, and beyond—I engaged with people and places I had only seen in movies. Each fall, I set off on the road to recruit the next class. I met with students in their high schools, at college fairs, and with community-based organizations. I gave speeches about applying to college and sang the praises of my beloved alma mater. Some days, my time was spent interviewing students. I learned about their hopes and dreams, their struggles and regrets. Along the way, I met some of their parents and made deep connections with my colleagues on "the other side of the desk," high school counselors.

I would then return to campus for what those of us in the business call "reading season." Reading admission files was like taking a daily trip around the globe. One day I was evaluating files from India and South Africa, and the next day, Bakersfield and Tacoma. The intellectual rigor of calculating grade point averages (GPAs), understanding high school curricula, and evaluating test scores in the context of a student's lived experience was exhilarating. Every time I opened a file (they were paper files back then), I was transported to a different world. With each student, I felt like I was putting together pieces of a puzzle. My goal was to understand the student, their readiness for college, and their fit with my institution.

After we read all the files, my colleagues and I would sit in an admission committee to build the first-year class. We always had more student applications than we had openings, so the committee process felt tense but also incredibly exciting. This is where the admission team came together to tell stories about the students they most wanted to admit and make trade-offs to meet institutional goals. I learned so much in admission committee and, each year, couldn't wait to do it again.

The most exciting part of the year was when we admitted students who decided to enroll, and we greeted them and their families at first-year orientation. To witness the hope and joy of a family as they arrive on campus and know you played a role in their journey (perhaps you were even the deciding vote on their admission application)—there is no greater high.

There is a saying in the college admission counseling profession—"three or thirty." It means if you stay longer than three years, you will become a "lifer" in this field. I love this work, and more than a quarter of a century later, I'm thrilled to still be in the profession. After serving in admission, enrollment, and student success roles on college campuses for more than two decades, including two deanships, I am honored to serve as the CEO of the National Association for College Admission Counseling (NACAC). NACAC is the largest association in the world for college access professionals. Our mission is to empower college admission counseling professionals through education, advocacy, and community. This is the mission that guides my work and part of the reason I've chosen to write this book.

Admission officers play a significant role in shaping our society. My own life was changed by an admission officer, and I have had the honor of paying it forward thousands of times as an admission dean. The role and impact of these leaders are too important to allow them to just "wing it." They deserve strategic cultivation, mentorship, support, and guidance. It is why I do this work and why I have written this book.

Despite the extraordinary meaning and purpose these roles have given me, I am fully aware the deanship has become more difficult to navigate. The role of NACAC CEO has given me an even deeper lens into the lives of admission professionals across the globe. I frequently communicate with admission leaders, and I will admit I am distraught by the loss of joy they experience in their roles today. Many are leaving the profession, and those who stay are burned out. Their voices and experiences have inspired me to write this book.

The work of admission deans is critical for the success of our nation. We need strong and healthy leaders to thrive in these roles. There are direct correlations between nations with high levels of educational attainment and economic prosperity, civility, and individual health.[2] The act of enrolling students in college depends on admission officers, yet most of us stumble into this profession with little training and climb the ranks toward leadership with a "sink-or-swim" mindset.[3] There is too much at risk to allow this lack of preparation to be the standard any longer.

I still believe serving as an admission counselor is one of the most joyful jobs in the world. I'm also keenly aware the headwinds facing higher education today make moving "up the ladder" into admission leadership roles extremely challenging. In my role as NACAC CEO, I meet regularly with admission deans to ask questions and "take a pulse" of the state of the profession. One of my inspirations for writing this book was a comment I heard over and over again from these leaders: "'Joy' is no longer the word I would use to describe this job." Almost every dean I meet with is struggling to find joy in the role. Many are considering leaving the field, some have been fired, and others hang on in misery. Most admit that, by staying, they are making incredible sacrifices to their own mental and physical health.

It takes tremendous courage to lead in college admission today. There is no shortage of challenges facing higher education—campus protest controversies, financial pressure, political scrutiny, and much more—and they all land at the doorstep of the admission dean in one way or another.[4] Our profession must be more intentional in preparing deans for success—not just for their own health, but also the college's. Without the admission office, there are no students. Without students, there is no revenue. Without revenue, there is no college.

I have always argued that the mission of the college begins in the admission office. How you craft your first-year class and whom you invite into your community are how you manifest your mission. Yet, I do understand that colleges and universities cannot be successful unless the admission office brings in enough students to meet the college's goals—most important, its revenue goals.[5] As the book *Mission and Money: Understanding the University* reminds us—there is no mission without money.[6]

The headwinds buffeting today's admission deans are strong. One of the greatest pressures of leading an admission office is its outcomes are very public and very easy to scrutinize. Satyajit Dattagupta, executive vice chancellor, chief enrollment officer, and senior advisor to the president at Northeastern University, is keenly aware of this. "There is nowhere to hide in this role. My success and failure will be very transparent," he told me."[7] Unlike the work of other offices on campus whose operations are often broadly focused on student development and the academic mission, admission has quantifiable targets it must reach each year. The data are usually publicly available, and most community members are aware of the annual enrollment targets.

Muriel Poston is a former colleague and dean of faculty at Pitzer College, where I served as vice president and dean of admission and financial aid. Muriel described the enrollment and net tuition revenue goals I was given by the president each year as "landing a jumbo jet on a tiny runway. There is no room for error."[8] If the admission team doesn't hit their targets for a first-year class—if enrollment is low, or the balance is off—staff layoffs may follow, or perhaps staff will receive no raises that year.[9] Fury from the community often ensues. For instance, if you work at a highly selective college and the community cares deeply about rankings, a drop in the average GPA or test scores of your entering class could send trustees, donors, and alumni into upheaval (despite some rankings agencies moving away from these factors). If you overspend your financial aid budget or don't generate enough net student revenue, the college budget could go into a deficit, and the bond ratings agencies might lower the institution's credit ratings. If you overenroll the class, the student affairs staff may be frustrated because they don't have enough beds, and faculty members may be angry because their first-year seminar class sizes are too large. If you don't bring in a diverse enough class, protests may ensue about the college's commitment to diversity. I still remember the year Jewish student enrollment dropped at my previous institution. Campus Hillel leaders, donors, alumni, and Jewish students were outraged. The list of people you may anger with enrollment outcomes is endless, and they all have valid reasons for challenging your decisions as an admission leader.

The experienced admission leader will note that none of the challenges I mention are new. The profession has grappled with these issues for decades. What has made the work of a chief enrollment officer even more challenging are the external headwinds they currently face. The title of an article in *The Hill* captures what most enrollment leaders are feeling today: "Higher Education's Perfect Storm Is Becoming a Tsunami."[10] I began writing this book six months after the US

Supreme Court decision that struck down the use of race in college admissions and only a few days after the presidents of Harvard, the University of Pennsylvania, and eventually Columbia stepped down from their posts after a horrific takedown that has left many of us in the profession gutted.[11]

As I write this book, enrollment leaders are facing more challenges than ever. Fewer births during the last recession have resulted in fewer high school students in the pipeline to college.[12] This "demographic cliff" has increased competition between institutions for students, all while the number of families with the ability to pay full tuition is shrinking.[13] I still remember when I first became an admission dean, the CFO would say to me, "Just bring me a few more students who can pay to help me balance the budget." Although it was still a big ask back then, tuition was lower, and more families could afford the entire cost. Today, with private college tuition averaging $38,431 and public college tuition averaging $19,024 per year, most families today need a significant amount of financial aid to afford college.[14] If you add the cost of room and board, the fees get even more unattainable. The median household income in the US is $80,610, making it nearly impossible for most families to afford today's tuition prices. In fact, more than 87 percent of students today receive some form of aid.[15] Despite this financial assistance, the total average student loan debt is still $40,681.[16]

It is no wonder admission deans find themselves in a conundrum. As Brian Rosenberg, president emeritus of Macalester College, writes in his most recent book, *"Whatever It Is, I'm Against It": Resistance to Change in Higher Education*, "When the service you provide costs more than people are willing and able to pay for it, when you are unable to lower the cost of that service, and when the number of your potential customers is shrinking, you have what one might describe as an unsustainable financial model."[17]

Yet the financial model is only part of the challenge facing admissions deans today. During the pandemic, more than a million students chose not to go to college, accelerating our drop over the enrollment cliff.[18] In 2024, technical glitches with the new Free Application for Federal Student Aid created major challenges for students and institutions, and many institutions reported enrolling fewer students as a result.[19] If you add legislation opposing diversity, equity, and inclusion practices in various states; increased legal scrutiny of higher education; campus protest controversies (which some institutions have reported negatively impacted their enrollment); and rhetoric by politicians and the media that higher education isn't worth the cost, it's no wonder many Americans are losing confidence in higher education. As a result, leading an admission office has never felt more tumultuous.[20]

It isn't surprising the high-energy, optimistic admission officers who began their careers with so much hope and joy are choosing not to move into the top admission role. Those with the courage to lead are burned out and leaving the profession faster than expected.[21] According to *The Chronicle of Higher Education*, heads of admission have remained in their jobs for only a median of three years (and those that report to them—coordinators and counselors—have remained on the job for only a median of two years).[22]

Several admission deans have confided they have had significant health issues as a result of their job. One told me they had a heart attack, and another told me they had significant mental health challenges because of the extraordinary pressure. Another, who has witnessed many deans lose marriages or partnerships, told me, "This is a widower's profession."

Success in the admission deanship isn't just about managing the duties of the job—it's also about managing ourselves. Thriving in the role will require intentionality, both professionally and personally. It takes courage to lead, but it also takes skill and self-management—all of which can be learned. The challenge with the college admission counseling profession is that the skills we learn as we "grow up" in the field as admission officers don't necessarily prepare us for the complexities of the deanship. Excelling at recruitment, public speaking, application evaluation, daily operations, and program planning is critical for the success of admission counselors.[23] However, the deanship requires an entirely different set of skills and ways of operating.

I still remember moving from director to vice president during my time at Pitzer College, a member of The Claremont Colleges in Southern California. My main responsibilities as a director were managing a team of counselors, ensuring the internal operations of the office were flowing smoothly and making sure my recruitment and application evaluation territories were well attended to. After the retirement of the vice president who hired me, I was promoted into that role. Even though I was serving the same institution, the new job felt like I had landed on another planet. I immediately began reporting to the president, managing multimillion-dollar tuition revenue goals, navigating the politics of the board of trustees and the alumni board, attending faculty senate meetings (where admission was always a hot topic), answering calls from the media, balancing complex financial aid budgets, and spending a significant amount of time with the CFO, human resources director, and legal counsel. The memories of spending my days visiting high schools and meeting with hopeful students felt distant. I was now meeting with more disgruntled constituents than I could've ever imagined. I went from spending my days with joyful students and their families to contending with the mixed emotions and expectations of many top campus leaders. I was now a member of the president's cabinet, which meant I no longer just managed admission. I now advised the president, and together the cabinet and I helped guide the institution through daily challenges and opportunities.

In my experience, most people are never fully prepared for the onslaught of responsibilities and politics the deanship brings, and neither was I. I was fortunate to have wonderful mentors around me who helped me navigate this new territory. It also helped that I am energized by challenging roles and have always had a knack for thriving in chaos. My friends remind me that, although most people run away from burning buildings, I always seem to run toward difficult situations. I admit, I've been fortunate. Although my time in the admission deanship was certainly challenging, I was able to thrive, and I found an incredible amount of joy in the work. My success often came at a cost to my own personal life and health (which I will discuss more throughout this book), and now I realize it didn't have to be that way. Most newly appointed admission deans tend to sink or swim. Given the unprecedented pressures they now face, many are sinking. New ways of preparing for and operating in the role can change that.

My intention in writing this book is to provide sitting and aspiring deans with a roadmap for success. No book can prepare a dean for all the issues they will face in the role, but my goal is to shed light on important skills and strategies you can employ to succeed in the role—regardless of the type of institution you serve. Although admission leaders cannot control the external forces that impact their role, they can control how they respond to and navigate its complexity. I will share some of my own experiences and lessons learned as a leader in the field, and I will also share the work of some of the most successful admission deans in the United States. Each chapter contains voices from admission leaders at a set of diverse institutions.

In the first chapter, I share suggestions for how to choose a deanship, including what questions to ask yourself and what questions to ask the institution. Given the turnover in the role today, there is no shortage of jobs available, but selecting the right one is critical. In the second chapter, I provide guidelines for what to consider (and critical questions to ask) when transitioning into a role, how to design your first year, and how to build a high-performing team. In chapter 3, I focus on the importance of storytelling as a tool for cultivating change on your campus. In chapter 4, I discuss how to navigate complex politics in a shared governance system. In chapter 5, I share strategies for leadership in crisis. I complete the book by discussing an area of leadership I believe is the foundation of all success: managing and caring for yourself.

In each chapter, I also highlight leadership best practices drawn from the literature within and outside of higher education. Although higher education faces unique challenges, we can learn a lot from leaders in other nonprofit spaces, as well as corporate America. In fact, some of my own leadership philosophies have been informed by leaders outside of higher education, including restaurateurs Danny Meyer and Will Guidara and Disney CEO Bob Iger, whom you will hear more about in this book.

The future of college access and workforce development in the United States depends on strong leaders in higher education. I believe the college admission deanship can be rewarding and even joyful, but it must be cultivated with great care and intention. I'm convinced the next generation of leaders will transform the profession, and unlike many of us who began this work many years ago, they will have much more access to guidance and mentorship along the way. If you are a sitting or aspiring admission dean, I hope you will approach this book with an open heart and mind.

My intentions for the book are twofold. For aspiring deans, if the content of this book energizes and excites you, I hope you will answer the call to serve, because the admission deanship is indeed for you. As NBA star Magic Johnson reminded an audience of more than seven thousand NACAC members at our annual conference in 2024, "Each of you changes lives. You have been called to do this work."[24] If you are currently a dean, I hope this book provides you with tools, strategies, and inspiration to not just survive but thrive. And when you do, I hope you will pay it forward by preparing the next generation of leaders.

An important note—the term *admission dean* is used throughout the book to represent the role of chief enrollment and chief admission officers. In today's higher education landscape, titles vary widely from chief enrollment officer to dean of admission, vice provost for enrollment, chief admission officer, executive director, and more. Some leaders oversee admission and financial aid offices; some only oversee admission. Many university presidents and provosts are also expanding the portfolios of admission deans to include communications, marketing student success, career services, and more.[25] Although the titles and portfolios vary widely by institution, the leadership skills and strategies highlighted in this book are applicable throughout the wide variety of leadership roles in our diverse higher education landscape.

CHAPTER 1

Preparing for Success: Selecting a Deanship

Before choosing a deanship, you need to do some serious introspection. What is my purpose for being in this work? What are my values? How do those align with the institution? How does the institution describe their values, and what do they lean on when they have to make difficult decisions?

—Whitney Soule, vice provost and dean of admissions, University of Pennsylvania

If you decide that a college admission deanship is the right professional journey for you, the most important decision you will make is choosing which institution to serve. Institutions have different missions, values, goals, and histories. Ensuring all these align with your own values as well as your personal and professional goals is critical. I have found that professionals are often enamored with the idea of the top job but don't have a clear understanding of what the role requires. It's critical to research the institution and its leadership. When you take on the top role, you will live and breathe the institution; these roles are all encompassing. You will be one of the most visible brand ambassadors for the college or university. If you don't feel deeply connected to the mission, vision, and leadership of the organization, you run the risk of having a short leadership tenure. As Shirley Collado, president emeritus of Ithaca College, advises her higher education mentees: "Do your research, because if you are going to serve in a leadership role at a college—whether it's a cabinet member, the president, or a trustee—you have to love the institution."[1] Will Guidara, author of the book *Unreasonable Hospitality*, also notes that wherever you choose to work, you need to feel a sense of passion: "No matter what you do, it's hard to excel if you don't love it."[2]

There are several important factors to consider before choosing a deanship.

Key Factors and Considerations for Choosing a Deanship

1. Find the right fit.
2. Choose your boss wisely.
3. Research the data.
4. Don't be afraid of the portfolio.
5. Understand the politics.

In this chapter, we walk through each of these crucial factors one by one, unpacking relevant considerations as well as practical guidance and suggestions from my own experience and the experiences of sitting admission leaders. We'll end with what I call "Advice from the Deans," a roundup of forward-looking insights from some of the leading admission professionals across the country.

FIND THE RIGHT FIT

All deanships are not created equal. Managing enrollment at the University of Michigan, where you are processing approximately ninety thousand applications, navigating one of the most competitive athletic recruitment programs in the nation, and negotiating the demands of a state legislature is going to be different than managing enrollment for a small, private, tuition-driven liberal arts college.[3] Both require similar skill sets for success, but the day-to-day experience is going to be very different. Some admission officers choose small colleges because they find the most joy in being close to the student experience and engaging deeply with the life of a close-knit campus. Others want to manage large, complex operations because they get their joy from managing systems. They love the culture of Division I athletics and wrestling with state politics. Other professionals are passionate about promoting the regional university experience, while still others find the community college sector to be most rewarding. Before you decide which sector and institution to serve, you must be clear about your "why."

Fumio Sugihara, dean of admissions and financial aid at Hampshire College, believes exploring the "why" and finding the right fit will be most critical to your success. During his own search process, he asked himself, "Does the institution align with my own values? Can I be myself here?" For Fumio, who served a variety of different institutions throughout his career, he knew it was important to be at an institution that allowed him to be creative. He asked himself, "Who am I, and how does the culture of the institution fit my personality? How do the institution's goals align with my own unique skill sets?" His introspection did not steer him wrong. Despite serving several institutions with significant enrollment challenges and one that was threatened by closure, he admits, "I'm the happiest I've ever been."[4]

Similarly, Joseph Montgomery has served two historically black colleges—first Tuskegee University and then North Carolina A&T. As he did his own soul searching about where he wanted to be dean, he asked himself, "Who do I want to serve? What are the characteristics of the institution and what are the characteristics of the student body?" Montgomery was adamant he wanted to feel passionate about coming to work every day by serving a student population that represented his own background.[5]

It is critical that you ask yourself these kinds of questions before embarking on the road to the admission deanship because a good fit sets you up for success. In fact, this is something you may already know or have seen play out as an admission officer. When I was an admission officer, I would advise prospective college students to do some soul searching before choosing a college, because finding "fit" is most important and will determine whether they will have a good experience. I now advise admission professionals to do the same. You certainly don't have to serve the same kind of institution where you attended undergrad, but you must be clear-eyed about how other schools differ. One way to do your research is to

> Before you accept the job, you need to figure out if you and the president are speaking the same language. You must be on the same page because when things get tough (and they will), you need to make sure this person has your back.[6]
>
> —Lee Coffin, vice president and dean of admissions and financial aid at Dartmouth College

interview colleagues at various institutional types that are different from the ones where you have served. I highly recommend shadowing a colleague at an institution very different from the one you are most familiar with. It may give you a sense of how different kinds of institutions function and which operations might energize you the most. You would be surprised how different the challenges are, even for someone serving in a similar role. A day in the life of an admission dean at a small, private women's liberal arts college like Scripps College promises to be very different than at large, public institutions like the University of Connecticut or a multi-campus system like San Jacinto Community College.

CHOOSE YOUR BOSS WISELY

Most admission deans report to the president of the institution or the chief academic officer. The key to your success will be the relationship with your supervisor. In fact, this relationship can make or break your deanship. Joseph "J. T." Duck, dean of admissions at Tufts University, emphasizes the importance of choosing your boss wisely. "Make sure you are going to work for someone who is going to set you up for success," he says. "Choose a boss who is a mentor and coach, and someone who will support you when the going gets tough."[7]

In today's challenging landscape, presidents and provosts are feeling extraordinary pressure to meet enrollment and net tuition revenue goals.[8] Their success depends on your ability to meet the institution's targets. This requires a lock-step alignment that is difficult to cultivate if you're not on the same page. I find the reason many admission deans fail is because they are misaligned with their leaders. So often, I hear deans say, "My president just doesn't get it. She has unrealistic goals. She doesn't have my back." That may all be true, but I believe these conflicts should have been uncovered and addressed during the research and interview phase. Your employer's mode of operating—and their expectations for you as admission dean—should not be a surprise when you arrive on campus.

The interview for an admission deanship must go both ways. As much as the institution is interviewing you to make sure you are the right person for the job, you are interviewing your supervisor to make sure they are the right fit for you.

I asked several deans across the country what questions they feel are most important to ask their potential supervisor. These questions were consistent across all interviews:

- **What does success in this role mean to you?** It's important to be on the same page with your supervisor regarding outcomes and measurement of your success.
- **What are your goals for enrollment, and what kind of resources are you willing to provide the team to achieve them?** It's important to compare the enrollment goal to the fiscal resources you will be given to do the work. Will you have enough resources to hire a team, invest in technology, and so on?
- **Prior to my arrival, what was the perception of the admission/enrollment office on campus, and how would you like to see that evolve?** This will help you get a sense of the tone on campus. If the reputation of the admission office is poor, one of your first goals will be to rebuild trust on campus.
- **When the going gets tough (and it will), how will you have my back?** You may want to ask for examples of how this person has supported their direct reports during difficult times in the past. I've known many deans who were immediately fired when they did not meet their enrollment target. You don't want to put yourself in that situation.
- **How do you navigate crisis?** Grace under fire is an important leadership quality, and you want to explore whether this person has that trait.
- **How will you support my professional development?** Even though you have reached the top of your field, you will need to continue to grow. Explore what kind of resources the institution has for executive coaching, continuing education, and so on.
- **How can I help move your agenda forward?** This reminds your supervisor that you are there to ensure they meet their goals.

The last question is critical. I am often amazed at how many deans don't realize that their number one job is to partner with their supervisor to move their agenda forward. Although it's certainly healthy to challenge your supervisor on how those goals might be achieved, before you sign on the dotted line, you must know their agenda. The goals must be clear, and once you say "yes" to the job, you must be fully committed to helping your supervisor be successful. It is your North Star and top priority.

Marjorie Hass, a two-time college president and current president of the Council of Independent Colleges, reminds us that before taking a job, the first question you should ask is: "What is the problem I am being asked to solve?"[9] So often, admission deans confess to me they knew the enrollment goal was too ambitious before they took the job. They hoped they could make it work or convince the community otherwise once they arrived on campus. During the interview, it's important to understand exactly what the goals and aspirations of the institution are, because if you accept the job, you are agreeing to fulfill them. So after you meet with all of the constituents on a campus and before you take the job, ask yourself, "What is the problem I'm being asked to solve?" If you feel you can solve it, and the challenge energizes you, then this is the right fit. If not, run for the hills.

One other important question to ask yourself is, "What levers can you pull at the institution?" Two-time vice president of enrollment D. J. Menifee asked himself this before he accepted a deanship. "Enrollment management in today's competitive environment is about trade-offs," he explains. "So, before you take on the deanship, you have to do your research to see if the institution has various levers that you can pull to meet enrollment goals. Is all of the tuition revenue driven by traditional undergraduate students, or do you have online and graduate programs that you can grow or expand? Are there unique strengths and differentiators on the campus that could help you grow enrollment? You will need as many creative options as possible to succeed."[10]

Finally, you want to choose a supervisor whom you can learn from. Whether you have served as a dean before, or this is your first leadership role, you will want to expand in your own professional growth, and to do so, you need to work closely with someone whose leadership you respect.

It's also important to acknowledge that the roles of college presidents and provosts are increasingly complex. In fact, a *Chronicle of Higher Education* article described the presidency as the hardest job in America.[11] Given the extraordinary challenges presidents and provosts currently face and the fact many don't last long in these roles, I agree. So, you want to choose a leader with a record of leading with courage, of being kind to their teams, who exhibits grace under fire, and who will have your back when the going gets tough.

To this end, I advise you to do as much research as possible on your future boss. One of the ways you can do that is by reaching out to someone who has worked with this person before. I've learned that, although higher education is a huge sector, our community feels small. In my experience, higher education is not six degrees of separation; it's more like two. In fact, before accepting the job as vice president for enrollment and student success at Trinity College, I did my research on the president, Dr. Joanne Berger-Sweeney, by speaking to those who worked for her in the past. She previously served as dean of the School of Arts and Sciences at Tufts University and as an academic associate dean at Wellesley College prior to that. I called colleagues we had in common and asked as many questions as I could about her leadership style, her ability to support her team, her temperament, and, most important, whether they thought she was kind. Kindness is one of my most important values, and a leader who does not exhibit it would not be a good fit for me. You should make sure your values align with your supervisor. If they don't, I assure you, you won't last long in the job.

To my delight, everyone raved about Joanne and couldn't contain their excitement for her ascent to the presidency. Doing that research was time well spent. When I was on campus for my interview, I experienced firsthand how thoughtful and kind she was. After a whirlwind day full of meetings, I was sitting in my room at the campus inn and my cell phone rang. Joanne said, "I realize you are staying overnight on campus and are all by yourself. Would you like to come over and have dinner with my family?" I couldn't believe that a college president would take the time out of her busy schedule to check in on me and invite me to dinner. I thought her offer was incredibly kind and showed she led with her heart.

I eventually took the job and became one of Joanne's closest partners. She lived up to her reputation of being a courageous and heartfelt leader. She also kept her promise of always having my back when things got tough on campus—and believe me, they did (more on that a little later). Working for Joanne was like watching a master class in leadership. I'm convinced I learned more from her in five years than I would have in a leadership master's program. We didn't always agree, but she always pushed me to grow and challenge my own boundaries. Despite my eventual departure for the National Association for College Admission Counseling (NACAC), we have remained friends, and I still rely on her good counsel today. Choosing the right boss can be a transformative experience, so I implore you not to make the decision lightly. With the right boss, you will grow, you will thrive, and you will find joy.

RESEARCH THE DATA

I rarely use the word *never*, but when it comes to this topic, it is critical for me to do so. You should NEVER take a deanship without digging into the institution's enrollment data. If you take the job, you will immediately become responsible for the institution's data, so you need to know what you are walking into. The minute you become a finalist for the role, ask the president or provost to provide you with as much data about the institution as possible. First, you should look at the obvious data points (historic number of applications, yield, melt, and enrollment, and census data). Then, you need to go deeper.

You should ask the president or provost:

- What percentage of the institution's revenue is dependent on tuition?
- What is the net tuition revenue target each year, and how often has the goal been met?
- Historically, what has the discount rate been, and what is the goal today?
- How large is the financial aid budget, and how well has it been managed?
- Does the institution use merit aid as a strategy, or is all financial aid need based?
- Who is your peer group and whom does the institution compete with?
- Do you believe you are in the right peer group?
- What are the institution's bond ratings?
- What does the most recent accreditation report say about admission and enrollment?

And don't just stop with data about admission and financial aid. In order to succeed, you must know the entire picture. Jon Boeckenstedt, the vice provost for enrollment management at Oregon State University and author of *Data Stories Blog*, gives this advice:

> Data and trends are important, but it's seldom that numbers will tell you the whole story. The first thing I'd try to understand is whether this is a data-oriented culture: When people talk about the institution, do they agree on the numbers? You'd be surprised to learn how many people think differently about enrollment

> on campus, for instance. You might hear "enrollment is up," "enrollment is down," and "enrollment is steady" from three people, all who might be right in context.
>
> Second is some common understanding about why the numbers are the way they are. The "why" is almost as important as the "what" in many cases. Finally, are people sensitive to the duality of data? There are internal trends, of course, but unless that reality and the institutional aspirations are measured against external market realities, there can be trouble ahead for the enrollment person who's expected to fix or even just maintain the numbers.[12]

Many of the data points that tell an institutional story can be found in the Department of Education's Integrated Postsecondary Education Data System (IPEDS), but you will need to ask for the most current data possible. In fact, a meeting with the head of institutional research during your interview on campus may prove helpful. In addition, you may want to ask for data from the econometric model of the institution. Many institutions have a model they use to predict how many students will enroll, how much revenue they may achieve, and how much financial aid they will spend. Some will outsource this function to higher education firms, whereas others will host them in their institutional research (I.R.), financial aid, or business offices. The enrollment model is where the truth about enrollment success and challenges lie. The model will show you not just how many students apply and enroll but also what sort of financial complexities you may inherit.

Fumio Sugihara of Hampshire College states that digging into the data is the most important thing you can do before accepting a deanship. "The data always tells you the real story. When I was applying for a deanship, I literally created folders of data research: IPEDS, College Board, *US News*, and anything else I could get my hands on," he recalls. "It helps me understand who the institution is, and I compare that data to who they tell me the institution aspires to be. This is so important, because if the data doesn't support their aspirations, you may be setting yourself up for failure."[13]

D. J. Menifee, who served as vice president for enrollment at Susquehanna University in Pennsylvania and as vice president for enrollment, marketing, and communications at Bradley University in Illinois, also encourages aspiring deans to research where the institution sits in the marketplace: "Who are the institution's competitors? Are those competitors realistic, or is the peer group unrealistic? What are the levers the institution can pull to meet its goals? What are the institution's unique strengths?" Remember, the minute you take the job, it doesn't matter who came before you or how much of a challenge you've inherited—it's your responsibility now. Do your research and know what you're walking into."[14]

Finally, you will also want to ask to review the institution's most recent accreditation report. You will find important information about many of the institution's strengths and challenges, including enrollment. These are all highly confidential documents, so I would not ask for them unless you are at the very final stages of the search and are seriously considering taking the job. However, I must provide you with an important warning: do not accept the deanship without these important data. There are many surprises you will find upon your arrival to campus. The institution's data should not be one of them. Being aware of what you are walking into will ensure a much smoother transition.

DON'T BE AFRAID OF THE PORTFOLIO

As you embark on the search for a deanship, you will find that many admission deans are asked to oversee other departments. This is one of the reasons some directors are hesitant to move into the chief enrollment officer role. However, prospective deans should know that portfolio expansion is typical. Although it can seem intimidating to be responsible for an area you've never worked in, know it's an incredible opportunity for growth, and with the right preparation, you will thrive.

The most typical area that admission deans oversee is financial aid. The majority of institutions "house" these two divisions together. It makes perfect sense. Without financial aid, most students can't enroll at the institution. The two areas must work closely together to meet enrollment goals. These two offices typically collaborate on financial aid optimization, which, according to the higher education marketing firm Carnegie, is defined as: "the use of predictive models to determine each student's likelihood of enrolling at the institution and how institutional grant and scholarship awards affect that probability. Understanding the relationship between net cost and yield ensures that institutions can focus their limited aid resources on critical enrollment goals like headcount, net tuition revenue, and cohort composition."[15]

I strongly urge aspiring deans to get involved with financial aid before they apply for the role. Although you don't have to know how to package a student's aid award, you need to understand big-picture issues in financial aid. But you can start small. You might volunteer to staff financial aid events, then perhaps partner with a financial aid officer on scholarship programs. Ask to attend some of their meetings and join them at a local or national conference. You may want take financial aid certificate courses through organizations like the National Association of Student Financial Aid Administrators (NASFAA) or NACAC. Becoming a student of financial aid pays dividends when you enter the deanship. Although you don't have to be an expert, knowing as much as you can before becoming a dean will make your transition easier and ensure a stronger working relationship with your institution's director of financial aid. As Joseph Montgomery, associate vice president for enrollment management at North Carolina A&T states, "Most of us did not grow up in financial aid, but you need to study it. No one is going to ask you to package a student, but you should have an understanding of the institution's financial aid philosophy, how financial aid helps meet enrollment goals, and what implications it has for the students you serve."[16]

Financial aid, however, is not the only division that admission deans oversee today. Some institutions have learned that enrollment and retention are deeply connected and must work together to ensure success. My last leadership position on a campus was vice president for enrollment and student success. In my portfolio, I oversaw admission, financial aid, institutional research, retention, and career development.

The success of each of these areas is deeply interdependent. The president felt strongly she needed a leader in the organization that was thinking about the entire life cycle of the student, from recruitment to graduation and beyond. The model was so successful, she expanded the portfolio after I left to include student affairs and athletics.

This model is growing, and a brief Google search will help you find the variety of portfolios that admission deans oversee. Don't be intimidated by an expanded portfolio. Here is an analogy I use with aspiring deans: A college president has never overseen every area of the college before ascending to the presidency. The CEO of a company has rarely ever worked in every department within the organization. So it's typical when you ascend to leadership that you will supervise areas that you are not an expert in. However, this kind of transition does require strategy. Here are a few guidelines to ensure your success:

- **Don't claim to be an expert:** In each of the areas you supervise, you will typically have a director. When you first arrive on campus, it is important you admit you are not an expert in their area and don't intend to be. The key to success is forming a strong working (and trusting) relationship with each of your directors so that you know how to support them in their work.

- **Become a chief advocate:** Your job as the leader of the division is to be a staunch advocate for the area, understand what the issues are, find synergies and alignment between the different offices, provide the resources they need, and empower teams to do their best work. When your teams feel like you have their backs, they will perform at their best.
- **Become a student again:** Although you don't need to understand the daily operations of each of your areas, it is important you understand the issues and trends. Join the professional organizations of each of the areas you oversee. When I became vice president for enrollment and student success at Trinity College, I joined the National Association Student Financial Aid Administrators (NASFAA), the National Association of Colleges and Employers (NACE), the Association for Institutional Research (AIR), and the American Educational Research Association (AERA). Try to attend at least one of their professional conferences each year. This will help you understand the current trends and issues and will give you deeper empathy for the work your staff is currently doing. Follow the topics in higher education media like *The Chronicle of Higher Education* or read the research trends in academic journals like the ones published by the ASHE (Association for the Study of Higher Education).
- **Find peers:** As more admission deans oversee expanded portfolios, it is important to find your peers. Reach out to others who have similar portfolios. Form groups that get together on a periodic basis to discuss trends, challenges, and opportunities. You will be amazed at how robust the network is and how willing your peers are to help you succeed in your role.

UNDERSTAND THE POLITICS

In his book *"Whatever It Is, I'm Against It,"* former Macalester College President Brian Rosenberg notes: "Higher education has more third rails than a train yard."[17] That was certainly my experience during my two decades on campus. Institutions of higher education are some of the most politicized organizations in the US with complex governance structures that must be navigated strategically.

Before you accept a deanship, you need to get a sense of the politics you are walking into. Every institution has admission-related politics, and they can get heated. During my time as a vice president at Trinity College, I learned that if I didn't pay close attention to the politics of the institution, I wouldn't last long in the role. My years there were rife with political challenges. There were faculty who opposed my proposal to move the institution to a test-optional policy and change the way we evaluated students. There were alumni who were afraid I might change the historical makeup of the student body by admitting a more diverse set of students. The staff and faculty were on edge about making sure I met net tuition revenue targets and did not overspend financial aid—their salaries were at stake. The coaches were concerned I might alter the college's historic commitment to student-athletes, which could impact their ability to win, which in turn could negatively affect the institution's reputation and fundraising goals. The development office was concerned that enrolling a larger number of low-income students would limit their ability to meet current fundraising goals. The trustees wanted to see their institution rise in prestige and wanted to see a stronger academic profile for each entering class. These were just a few of the many complexities to be politically navigated during my tenure at the college—and every constituency required a different strategy and approach.

As is typical, most of these concerns I was facing did not begin with my tenure. They stemmed from the institution's long and complex history, one that takes years to truly understand. But the good news is you don't have to be caught entirely off guard when you arrive on campus. Asking the right questions during the interview process will help unveil some of these institutional politics and prepare you for handling them.

In fact, this is really the first "test" of your relationship with your potential supervisor. Ask about the politics of the place. Posing some of these questions will help you understand what you are walking into:

- **When it comes to enrollment, what are the faculty most concerned about?** This will help you understand what issues you might need to address beyond net tuition revenue and enrollment targets. Some faculty may be concerned about the academic quality of the student body, its diversity, or preparation for the rigor of the curriculum.
- **What pleases alumni, trustees, and donors about the work of admission, and what would they like to see change?** This question helps you dig even deeper. Are there politics around legacy admission? What kinds of

students do donors and trustees want to invest in? What politics might you have to navigate?

- **What is the role of athletics at this institution?** Regardless of the athletics division of your institution, you must learn what are the expectations of coaches and how much weight the institution puts on winning games. This will help you understand the pressure you might get for admitting student athletes.
- **What is the relationship between development and admission?** Is there pressure to admit legacy students or wealthy families?
- **What do students say about their peers? What kind of students would they like to see enrolled in the future?** Develop a relationship with the president of the student government and attend their meetings a few times a year. Ask this important question to find out whether students feel satisfied with the culture of the student body or if it needs changing.
- **If you take the last two classes that admissions enrolled, what would you say were their impact on the community?** If admission has not met the enrollment targets, you may be walking into a situation where the community is angry. This isn't a reason to walk away from the job, but it's important to be aware of the politics you will have to navigate and the trust-building you will have to engender.
- **Are there any recent controversial incidents that I should be aware of?** It's important to understand the historical context that you will inherit.

I asked as many questions during my search process at Trinity College as the search committee asked of me. I also visited campus several times before I took the job, just to make sure I was making the right decision. When I began the job, most of the admission-related politics that arose were not a surprise. I wasn't even shocked at how harsh the faculty and alumni were each time I tried to create change or suggest new ideas. The president was honest with me from the start. "This is not an easy place. If you decide to come here, you better have thick skin," she said to me during my final campus visit. Given my appetite for leadership challenges, I was not deterred, but I received the truthful information I needed to make an informed decision. You should, too.

Finally, the most important political strategy to employ when you move into the deanship is building trust. Campuses are riddled with networks of informal relationships, and you must cultivate your own. If you build trusting relationships in advance, you can rely on that political capital when crisis hits. Kasey Urquidez, former vice president for enrollment management and dean of admissions at the University of Arizona, believes that "from the day you take on the deanship, you must be a relationship builder. The time to build relationships is not when you are in crisis. You must build allies and humanize yourself with key constituents. It will help you when the going gets tough."[18] Ken Anselment, former vice president for enrollment and communication at Lawrence University, shares a similar sentiment. He notes, "The minute you arrive on campus, reach out proactively to your fellow leaders at the institution. Ask questions and demonstrate interest in their work. The more you all know each other's challenges and opportunities, the more quickly you will coalesce as a team."[19] Building allies through trust is a theme you will hear more about in the following chapters.

Advice from the Deans

On Selecting a Deanship

When I asked deans across the nation about advice on how to choose a deanship, several themes were consistent: be introspective about where you are in your own life, select according to the institutions mission and values, be selective about the supervisor you work for, and make sure you are excited to serve the kinds of students who attend that particular institution.

> I never thought I was ready for the role, so make sure to surround yourself by trusted mentors who can help you decipher when you are ready. Also, be open to nontraditional paths to the deanship. I spent five years as director of college counseling at a high school before returning to higher education. In hindsight, it was wonderful preparation for the deanship. I'm a better admissions leader for having done that.
>
> —Joseph "J. T." Duck, dean of admissions, Tufts University[20]

When you transition to the deanship, one of the most unsettling realizations you make is that you are now the final decision maker. That can feel like a lot of pressure, so take your time making decisions. Not too much time of course, but it's important to feel good about the decisions you make. I don't want to be rash in making my decisions, so I give myself time—despite the pressure I might be feeling from others. I find that when I do, I make better decisions.

—Kasey Urquidez, former vice president for enrollment management and dean of admissions, University of Arizona[21]

When I was considering a deanship, I asked myself—where can I be creative? Where can I make the biggest impact? What institutions align with my personality?

—Fumio Sugihara, dean of admissions and financial aid, Hampshire College[22]

You really have to know yourself before you take on these roles. There are so many competing interests in our work that if you don't really have a sense of your own core values, of what you believe in, it's going to be difficult for you to manage.

—Whitney Soule, vice provost and dean of admissions, University of Pennsylvania[23]

Ask yourself, who do I want to serve? What is the difference I want to make in higher education? What brings me the most joy? Choosing a deanship is all about institutional fit. You have to believe in the mission, in the students, in the community. The work is an opportunity to serve. Do some serious introspection before you choose.

—Mark Steinlage, vice president for enrollment management, Rockhurst University[24]

CHAPTER 2

Transitioning to the Deanship and Building Your Team

People will support a world they helped create.
—Dale Carnegie, writer and teacher

Your first few months on a new job are a critical time to learn the ins and outs of the institution, cultivate relationships, form a strategy, and build your team (or shape the one you've inherited). As you begin this role, I encourage you to undergo a mindset shift. I want you to think of yourself as the CEO of a small organization within a larger one. The strategies that new presidents and CEOs use to lead their organizations are the same strategies you can use to run your teams. I will be sharing those in this chapter. As the dean, you are the leader of one of the most important engines of the institution. The entire community will be depending on you to cultivate high-performing teams and produce stellar outcomes. During your transition, everyone from your direct staff to the board of trustees will be watching. What you do in your first year will send a powerful message about what your leadership style is, what you value, and how you make decisions.

In this chapter, we first explore key activities that will help you successfully transition into the deanship, including embarking on a listening tour and gradually building a culture of hospitality among your staff. This best practice in corporate contexts can translate well to colleges and universities. I include a list of critical activities for your first three months on the job. Then, we transition to building a team. I'll walk through strategies to help you cultivate and lead a strong group of admission professionals. Throughout the chapter, we'll hear "Advice from the Deans" about their transition to the top job and how they built their own teams.

THE LISTENING TOUR

Every leader who takes on a new role should embark on a listening tour. Shortly after arriving on campus, you should announce you will be gathering feedback from as many constituents as possible. Before you make any changes, hire a team, or admit your first class, you must know the needs of the community. A listening tour will give you the historical context you need to make informed decisions. The insights will not only be critical for your success but also show the community you care.

I can't emphasize this enough. Early in your tenure, listening and building networks are going to be critical to your success. Lee Coffin, vice president and dean of admissions and financial aid of Dartmouth College, shares, "I spent my first few years at Dartmouth listening and friend building. Every time I met a new constituent, I would ask myself—friend, foe, or skeptic? Who are the people I am going to need to convert?"[1] In the deanship, you'll need to have a good sense of what the key institutional issues and politics are, and you can't do that without asking the community to help you learn.

A listening tour meets several objectives. It makes you visible and presents you to the community. It positions you as a leader who is willing to listen and learn. It allows people to feel heard. I am a firm believer that people will support what they help build: if you invite members of the community to advise you as you transition into the role, you have a better chance they will support the changes you will make in the future. J. T. Duck of Tufts University did a lot of listening when he arrived. He believes that "one of your key roles as the dean is to represent the institution as accurately as possible, and you can't do that unless you know the place well. When you first arrive, you've got to speak with as many people as possible, in their own spaces on campus, not in your office. It sends a powerful message when you show up on their turf. It says, 'I care.'"[2]

When you embark on your listening tour, invite representatives from every constituency you can think of—current students, alumni, trustees, cabinet members, faculty, and so on. Most important, don't invite just supporters—include the critics, too. One of my strategies for success has always been to invite to the table those who have complaints. You will always learn something from them if you are open to listening with humility.[3] And although I wasn't always successful in pleasing individuals with complaints, the majority of them thanked me for listening and for including them.

> Before you go on your listening tour, remember to inform your president of your intentions. It's not only a professional courtesy but it also shows the president you are strategic and inclusive in your leadership. There is a high likelihood the president also went on a listening tour at the beginning of their tenure. So, remind the president your goal is to dig deeper into the admission and financial aid issues the community cares about most. Using this approach can help build trust early in your relationship with the president.

One thing I've learned in my career is people want to be heard—especially on college campuses, where shared governance means everyone gets to contribute to forming a future vision for the institution.

Finally, don't forget to reach out to one of your most important constituencies during your listening tour—school counselors and college advisors. During both of my vice presidencies, I made sure to sit down with counselors who supported students in the transition to college process. I wanted to hear about their experiences with the institution and get advice on how to better engage their students. After all, they're the ones with the pulse on how students and their families feel about your institution, your admission process, and more. Just as a corporate CEO would conduct research to understand how consumers are engaging with their products, a dean of admission needs to understand how their most important customer—the student—feels about their product—the institution. In fact, if your institution does not have a counselor advisory board, you may consider creating one. This is an opportunity to form a small group of counselors who will help you keep an eye on trends that are key to your success—like how students and families make decisions about choosing a college and how they perceive your institution or your admission policies.

Once you complete your listening tour, it's important to produce a "findings" report that you share with the president, cabinet, and trustees. In the spirit of transparency, you should also share it with your staff. Depending on the institution and its shared governance model, you might also share it with faculty, the alumni board, and other campus constituents. It's important for people to know what you've learned and how their voices contributed to the final product. This will also begin a sense of shared ownership. When people have a clear sense of the challenges, it's easier to rally them around a cause.

Returning to this "findings" document frequently is also important. In my experience, members of a campus community tend to have short memories. So, when I implement changes or propose new policies and procedures, I often return to the findings report and remind the community I am delivering on the needs and desires they expressed during the listening tour. It's important to connect the dots (and you will hear more about this strategy in chapter 3 of this book).

Inevitably, your listening tour will result in an endless list of things to do, fix, or change. I would not rush to present all the solutions; the truth is, you won't have them yet. Your intention in sharing the outcomes of the listening tour is to find themes, highlight points of alignment, points of tension, and clear opportunities. This document, along with the goals of the president and board (and the institution's strategic plan), will be the roadmap for your work in the years ahead.

This is also a good time to emphasize that leaders must admit they don't have all the answers. In fact, some of the things you learn on your listening tour won't be your problems to solve. They may lie in the purview of other campus leaders. Your first job is to determine where you have control and where you have influence. Enrollment challenges are nuanced and complex, and they require creative solutions. You will feel pressured into solving all the challenges as quickly as possible. But it's impossible to do so, and if you try, you will quickly experience burnout. Instead, take the findings back to your team and build a realistic plan together. As former President of Pitzer College Laura Trombley (now president of Southwestern University) reminded me when she appointed me dean, "This job is a sprint, not a marathon. Run too fast, and you'll run out of steam. So pace yourself, because we need you for the long haul."[4]

I will admit I didn't take her advice. In fact, one of the criticisms both of the presidents I worked for (and my board chairs at the National Association for College Admission Counseling [NACAC]) had for me was that I moved too quickly.

They reminded me that most people don't work at my pace and that it often takes time to bring everyone along and build consensus. It has taken me many years and several leadership roles to learn the lesson that you can't solve all of the challenges you inherit in a year or so. Pace yourself and take the long view. Set realistic plans. What can you address in your first year, second year, in five years? This strategy will ensure your success while avoiding burnout.

Finally, you should revisit the findings of your listening tour every year. Review them with your team and ask, "Are we making progress on addressing the concerns we heard from the community?" As you begin to address each issue on campus, don't forget to keep pointing back to the document. This reminds your constituency you are not making decisions in silos, but rather, as a result of their input and counsel.

When I became NACAC CEO, I embarked on a listening tour with members from all over the globe. I wanted to know what their aspirations were for the organization and where they felt change needed to happen. I created an executive summary of the tour with clear themes we found. The results were shared with all of our constituents, and in fact, it lives on our website.

At every NACAC board meeting, I end my updates with a PowerPoint slide that summarizes the outcomes of the listening tour and where we are headed. Each year, at our annual conference, I also deliver a "state of the association" address. I make sure to remind our members about the themes of the listening tour and detail our steps to ensure we are moving in the right direction, delivering on our promise of operationalizing their goals.

Ken Anselment, former vice president of enrollment and communication at Lawrence University, believes a similar approach should be taken on campus. "This is a great approach with university trustees, as well. As dean, you are living in (and carrying) the day-to-day reality of the work, while trustees are often episodic in their focus on that work. And because most of them have their own full-time jobs to attend to, they don't always keep the important stories front of mind. Your job is to remind them what we talked about last time (and often the time before that) before pivoting to the present and future."[5]

When you embark on your own listening tour, ask one of your staff members to join you so that they can take notes. You want to be fully present in those meetings instead of glued to your notebook or laptop—you want people to feel like you are truly listening and engaging. However, you don't want to lose any details,

Your First Three Months on the Job

Your first few months on the job are about assessing the challenges and opportunities while learning the culture of the organization. Although you were hired to lead, your first three months on the job are about listening and learning. You don't want to move too fast and make decisions you will regret or ones that don't properly consider the culture and politics of the institution. In your first few months, you need to listen, assess, build coalitions, and work toward a strategy. In each of my own leadership transitions, I have used Michael Watkins's book *The First 90 Days* as a guide.[6] I have gifted the book to more leaders than I can count, and I hope you will consider using it as well. Below are the ten strategies he suggests using in your first ninety days, which I have used in every leadership transition I have made (and you will see mentioned in other sections of this book):

1. **Promote yourself:** How will you introduce yourself to the organization? What are the skills you will need to learn in this new job? Which are transferable from the last one? How will you need to operate differently in this new role to succeed?
2. **Accelerate your learning:** What system will you put in place to learn as much about the organization as you can? Who do you need to meet with and hear from? How do you begin to understand the culture (the things that are said and unsaid)? Who are the people in the organization that can help you best get up to speed on culture?
3. **Match strategy to situation:** How do you learn the history and the context of the institution (and your office) before you begin to create a strategy? Before you make any decisions about organizational structure or policy changes, how do you get up to speed on how the past might impact the future?
4. **Secure early wins:** What is some of the "low-hanging fruit" that might secure you an early win? How do you address some of the issues your president or provost are most concerned about early? How might you champion an issue your staff has been wanting the dean to deal with for a long time?

5. **Negotiate success:** How do you negotiate with your president or provost to create realistic goals that will set you and your team up for success?
6. **Achieve alignment:** How do your systems, culture, staff skill sets, and organizational strategy align to achieve your goals? If one of those areas is misaligned, it will be difficult to succeed.
7. **Build your team:** What are the skill sets you will need around you to ensure your goals are operationalized? Who are the right people to not just do the job but also promote the culture you aspire to?
8. **Create coalitions:** Who are the campus influencers and constituents you will need to build coalitions with in order to advance your agenda? Perhaps it's key faculty members, or the VP for communications, or the chair of the alumni board. At every institution it's different, but building coalitions is critical early in your tenure.
9. **Keep your balance:** How will you commit to taking care of yourself in this new role, set boundaries, and also remain calm in difficult moments? Managing yourself will be one of your greatest challenges, and learning to do so early in your tenure will pay off for years to come (see more in the self-management chapter of this book).
10. **Expedite everyone:** How do you help others on your team and across the campus expedite their own learning and understanding of the issues they must address, and how will you empower them to create their own strategies for success?

so having someone take notes for you is critical. It's also helpful to have someone to process each session with you afterward—to confirm what you've heard, catch what you may have missed, and validate conclusions. If the budget allows, retaining a consultant who can sit in on the sessions and produce the final report will help deter bias and conflicts of interest.

A Culture of Hospitality

> Everyone walks around wearing a sign that says, "Make me feel special."[7]
>
> —Danny Meyer, restaurateur

Some may find it odd I would write about hospitality in a book about college admission, but I firmly believe that, at our core, college admission is a business of hospitality. Whether we like it or not, students and their families are paying for a very expensive service; in fact, probably one of the most expensive investments of their life.

One of the most important strategies to employ when you transition to the deanship is to build a culture of hospitality. The admission office must be the most welcoming, comfortable, joyous, and accommodating place on campus. You are the front door to the institution, and every experience a prospective student and family has will make a difference in deciding whether they enroll.

This all sounds simple. It's Admission 101. Yet, I am in awe of how often I arrive at an institution and find unhospitable practices—like outdated processes where students have to call between 9 a.m. and 5 p.m. to set up a visit. (What happens to international students and students in different time zones?) Or I find admission officers who didn't go above and beyond to make special accommodations for a family who requested it.

I still remember one first-year orientation day when a family arrived an hour before our registration desk was open. I was standing next to a student affairs colleague, who was stressed about everything she had to get done that day. She yelled at the family, "We ain't open yet!" Here was a family who had flown across the country, hauling luggage (and by the way, they were also paying a hefty price in tuition and fees—one of the families that higher education refers to as "full pay"), and this is how we treat them? I was mortified! I immediately apologized, helped them with their bags, and offered to buy them a drink at our campus coffee shop.

As the enrollment leader on campus, you must instill a culture of hospitality. Start with your office and then try to infiltrate the rest of the campus. When I was an admission dean, I would tell our community we couldn't beat our competitors based on endowment, resources, or ranking—but we could in fact beat them on how we made students and parents feel. One of my favorite quotes from Maya Angelou is, "People will forget what you said, they will forget what you did, but they will always remember how you make them feel."[8] I had that quote laminated and gave it to each of my staff members. I wanted them to understand we were in the people business and our number one priority was to create extraordinary experiences for our students and their families.

In fact, if you have the opportunity to partner with someone in the hospitality industry to come and do a training for your team, that would be ideal. Perhaps you have an alum who works in the industry who can come talk about the hospitality mindset. I believe that hotels such as the Ritz Carlton and Four Seasons, as well as Disney, all have extraordinary hospitality trainings, as do some of the most successful restaurateurs in the world. One book I would suggest reading is *Unreasonable Hospitality: The Remarkable Power of Giving People More Than They Expect* by Will Guidara, whose training at some of the best restaurants in the world has helped him create a philosophy of hospitality that translates to any industry. In his inspirational book, he posits, "I believe that whatever you do for a living you can *choose* to be in the hospitality business."[9]

I cannot overstate it: during your transition, you must immediately begin to establish a culture of hospitality on your campus. Higher education is expensive, and families have a lot of choices. How you make them feel can be the difference between meeting your enrollment goals or not.

Advice from the Deans

On Transitioning into the Deanship

Every dean I interviewed felt that how well you transition into the role will determine how long you stay and how you succeed. It's clear that relationship building was one of the most important tasks in the first year. Each of them felt that the building of trust was the key to their long-term success.

> As a Dean, your number one priority is to help your boss (or bosses) know that you understand what their needs are, that they hired someone competent, and they can trust that you are here to support them in meeting those needs.
>
> —Joseph "J. T." Duck, dean of admissions, Tufts University[10]

> Even before you start the job, begin doing your research and establishing relationships. I call those pre-service days. Ask for data that you did not have access during your interview process, start digging deeper into the institution's data and history, and try to understand the politics of the

place as early as you can. That way, you can hit the ground running on day one.

—Delorean "D. J." Menifee, former vice president for enrollment, marketing & communications, Bradley University[11]

Follow through is SO important. When you start meeting with people on campus, you need to make sure you follow through with any promises you make, or circle back to the things you said you would research. It's tough because sometimes you will feel so overwhelmed with so many things to follow through on, but if you don't, you will lose their trust forever.

—Kasey Urquidez, former vice president, enrollment management, and dean, admissions, University of Arizona[12]

Set yourself up for an early win. It's so important. The path to May 1st is long, so you want to show success along the way. Whether its increasing inquiries or applications, or successfully administering an event—have something that your team and your colleagues at the college can celebrate.

—Satyajit Dattagupta, executive vice chancellor, chief enrollment officer, and senior advisor to the president, Northeastern University[13]

Earlier in my profession, I thought getting the work done was enough. But I now realize that building relationships matters greatly. As a dean, I spend the first year building strong relationships campus wide. I know that eventually I am going to need strong support to get my agenda accomplished, and the key to success is going to be those relationships.

—Joseph Montgomery, associate vice provost for enrollment management, North Carolina Agricultural and Technical State College[14]

It might feel counterintuitive, but in moments where you feel pressured, slow down. You are going to be asked to make a lot of decisions, and in the beginning, you won't have the entire context and nuance. In those moments, we all need to slow down and take an intentional pause. You'll always make better decisions as a result.

—Whitney Soule, vice provost and dean of admissions, University of Pennsylvania[15]

When you arrive on campus, read everything you can written or posted by students. Read the newspaper, check out the social media pages of clubs and organizations, and more. You've got to figure out how students perceive the institution, and what they care about.

—Fumio Sugihara, dean of admissions and financial aid, Hampshire College[16]

BUILDING YOUR TEAM

> The only way a company can grow, stay true to its soul, and remain consistently successful is to attract, hire, and keep great people. It's that simple, and it's that hard.[17]
>
> —Danny Meyer, restaurateur

Once you've settled into your role, the key to your success as an admission dean will be determined by the strength of your team. Most new admission deans inherit a team, but given the high turnover in the field, there are always opportunities to fill new roles.

I would never have been able to accomplish all the things I did in my various roles as an admission dean had it not been for the extraordinary teams I built and cultivated. You need to surround yourself with a group of people who are diverse in skill set, lived experience, and talent.

My secret weapon has always been to hire people who are smarter than me and who will challenge me. Many leaders do the opposite. They hire people they feel will tell them what they want to hear and will acquiesce to their whims. A true leader knows they need advisors by their side who bring the skills they don't have and who will respect them enough to push back when they feel they are making a bad decision. This is most important when leading in crisis (which will be discussed in chapter 5). Michael Sandler, a communications expert who works with university leaders, speaks directly to this issue in an *Inside Higher Ed* article: "Too many presidents reward vice presidents who simply validate their opinions. This role should not be that way. When you are on a sinking ship, you don't want someone telling you that you're a great captain. You want someone to show you where the life rafts are."[18]

I believe many deans do the same. Hiring people who are smarter than you requires an awareness of your own strengths—and, more important, your deficits. For example, I have never enjoyed the quantitative aspects of my job (despite the fact there have been many). I spent most of my undergraduate career in social science courses, and my PhD thesis focused on qualitative research. Yet, I knew that success in enrollment management required quantitative expertise. As a vice president, I was also responsible for managing multi-million-dollar budgets—so, having team members who could partner with me in these elements of the work has always been critical. I got as much training and mentorship on the quantitative aspects of the job as I could, but my success came from empowering people who truly enjoy quantitative work and could advise me in making the best decisions.

In addition, I'm a "big picture" person. I've never thrived in the operational weeds of any office. However, I am keenly aware that when leaders have a vision, strategy must be implemented and operationalized at every level. I've always surrounded myself with staff members who enjoy operations work. They are the ones who make the vision come to life and who also push back and let me know when an idea I come up with is just not realistic. The key, of course, is to take their sound advice and not allow egos to get in the way. My staff makes me uncomfortable all of the time—because they often disagree with me. They don't always share the news or feedback I want to hear, but it's important I cultivate an environment where they feel comfortable voicing their differing opinions. Because I've built trusting relationships with them and I know they are the experts in their respective areas, I am confident they have the best interests of the organization (and my leadership) at heart.

The first thing you, as a new dean, should do is to spend time understanding where their skill gaps lie and building a team of people who can fill those gaps. It takes courage to hire a team of people who are fundamentally different from you. They are the ones who see the potholes you can't and who will make you uncomfortable by pushing back when they feel you are headed in the wrong direction. These are the people who will be critical to your success.

Finally, before you officially begin to build your team, ask yourself—as a dean, what are the things that only I can do? The truth is, your teams can handle recruitment, file evaluation, and other operational tasks, but only you can manage relationships with the president, meet with donors, and deal with complex per-

Key areas to assess your strengths and knowledge gaps:

- Data analysis
- Budget modeling, forecasting, and reporting
- Public speaking
- Writing (for academics and the general public)
- Project management
- Media engagement
- Communications
- Financial aid and enrollment predictive modeling
- Information technology and customer relationship management (CRM)
- Research and analysis

sonnel issues. Reflecting on my experience as a dean of admission, I wish I had asked myself that question earlier in my career. It would have saved me a lot of time, energy, and burnout. Early on in my deanships, I made the mistake of trying to do my old job as an admission officer (e.g., visiting high schools, reading applications, speaking at high school events) while also doing my new one (e.g., managing the president's and trustees' goals, engaging alumni, navigating institutional politics, managing predictive enrollment modeling, and considering legal and human resources issues). I shouldn't have tried to do it all, and neither should you. If you are a new dean, think about the role you uniquely play as the dean. Do that job, and do it well. Build a great team and empower them to do the rest.

On Hiring

The former CEO of Porsche, Peter Schutz, is thought to have said, "Hire character, train skill."[19] Disney CEO Bob Iger would agree with him. He notes, "When hiring, try to surround yourself with people who are good in addition to being good at what they do. Genuine decency—an instinct for fairness and openness and mutual respect—is a rarer commodity in business than it should be."[20]

Satyajit Dattagupta of Northeastern University has a hiring philosophy that has served him well. He doesn't just focus on the skill set of a potential employee (which he calls "aptitude")—he also focuses on their emotional intelligence (which he calls "attitude"). "I am no longer willing to sacrifice on attitude," he explains.

"What's the point of hiring the smartest person on the planet if we are misaligned on values and the way we approach our work? I hire people who are teachable, motivated, curious, and eager."[21] In admission, attitude is critical. You may hire a counselor who can read and analyze applications, give a good presentation, or analyze data. But if they don't have a strong work ethic, or a natural inclination toward making students and families feel good by creating a culture of hospitality, they won't succeed in the role.

One of the US's most successful restaurateurs, Danny Meyer, has a similar hiring strategy, which he calls the 51 percent. When he hires at his company, 49 percent of what he looks for in an employee is the ability to complete tasks. Can they do the tactical side of the job? More importantly, he pays close attention to the remaining 51 percent—the emotional intelligence needed to go above and beyond the tactical side of the job. In his book *Setting the Table* (another phenomenal hospitality book), Meyer writes that he wants to hire people who "naturally radiate warmth, friendliness, happiness, and kindness."[22] This is why he hires people with the 51 percent, who he believes exhibit five core emotional skills:

- *optimistic warmth*: genuine kindness and thoughtfulness; a glass half-full
- *intelligence*: a genuine curiosity for learning
- *work ethic*: desire to do things in the best manner possible
- *empathy*: constant concern about how they make others feel
- *self-awareness and integrity*: accountability, honesty, and good judgment[23]

In my own experience, these are the skills that not only make a good hire but also create a joyful, trusting, and high-performing workplace. Employees care deeply about organizational culture, so hiring individuals because they have the skills to do the job is not enough to create a thriving organization. Your strategy for hiring teams must be based on the kind of culture you aspire to build.

On Cultivating a Team

Hiring the right team is the first step, but cultivating and retaining them are even more critical. If you are to succeed in the role, you must pay close attention to how you develop your team and ensure they are growing with you. College admission offices are infamous for their turnover, but this trend can be reversed if we pay attention to the reason why staff members leave.[24]

Hire Slow, Fire Fast

Although it's one of the hardest things you'll ever do, letting go of a staff member who is not up to the task is also critical to your success. In my experience, most institutions of higher education are hesitant to fire employees out of fear of retaliation or hurting feelings. The business of college admission is high stakes. If you have underperformers on your team, your outcomes will suffer, and team morale will decline. In fact, author Perry Belcher is credited with saying that "nothing will kill a great employee faster than watching you tolerate a bad one."[25] Keeping underperformers on the team sends a clear message to high performers: it doesn't matter if you don't work as hard as everyone else.

My philosophy has always been to be slow to hire and quick to fire. What I mean by that is you should take your time finding the right person for the job—the 51 percenter. Finding the right person is always worth the wait, so don't rush. However, when you have an employee who is clearly a bad fit and bringing down the morale of everyone else, you shouldn't keep them on the team for very long. Doing so will have a negative impact on other members of your team. It takes courage to move people along, but it could be the difference between success and failure. Just remember to always do it with kindness and grace. Clinical psychologist and Northwestern University professor Alexandra Solomon reminds us that "honesty without tact is cruelty." When delivering difficult news to an employee, "always separate the behavior from the person."[26] Although letting people go is hard, I've always shared the news in a way that honors the work they've done and contributions they've made to the organization. I firmly believer that, even when people are not a good fit for your organization, you allow them to exit with dignity.

You must invest in your staff's professional development and keep a pulse on what excites them most about the job. If your team feels you don't care deeply about their growth, they will find another supervisor who does. Today's leaders must get to know their staff members on an individual basis and find out what makes them "tick."

One of the things I do with my own leadership team is to ask each individual what motivates or energizes them at work. Some tell me they are motivated by praise; others tell me they are motivated by creativity; some enjoy complex problem solving. Understanding this about each team member allows me to tailor their work, present them with opportunities that energize them, and give them feedback in the ways they like to receive it. I believe that everyone wants to do a good job, and most people want to grow in their roles. But we must take the time to get to know each person on an individual basis and tailor their employment journey accordingly.

I find that asking my team members directly about their future goals and aspirations also helps me to create an individualized cultivation plan. If I know someone aspires to a leadership role, I try to add responsibilities each year that will give them the experience they need to get to the next level. If someone aspires to grow in a particular area of the organization, I give them the exposure they need. This will sometimes require moving away from traditional job descriptions and thinking creatively about an individual's portfolio. In my experience, shifting responsibilities so that a staff member can grow almost always leads to greater job satisfaction and commitment to the organization.

As NACAC CEO, I have implemented a new process with my staff members called *career conversations*. Unlike an annual performance evaluation, this conversation takes place mid-year and is focused on the employee's growth. It's an opportunity for team members to share information about their goals, aspirations, joys, and frustrations in the workplace. It gives staff members a platform to reflect on what's going well and what they wish could be different. Most important, it's an opportunity for supervisors to listen, learn, and empathize—three key factors I find are often missing in many organizations.

As a result of these career conversations, I have developed individualized strategies for each member of my leadership team. Some have received executive coaching, whereas others attended leadership training. Some pursued continuing graduate education, whereas others were given sabbatical time to work on important projects. Each person's area of focus was different, and so was the strategy I used to cultivate them. Taking the time to learn about our teams and invest in them strategically will be the key to their long-term success, as well as your own.

Questions to Consider for Career Conversations

1. I'd like you to review your position profile as it was written when you applied for (or were promoted into) your current role. As you read that description, what surprises you? What delights you? Does the position profile match what you expected and currently experience? If not, let's talk about that. I'd love to hear you reflect honestly on that position profile and how it's playing out in reality. How is it accurate? How would you update it?
2. The goal of any career should be to move toward the things that bring you most joy and energy. As you reflect on your day-to-day responsibilities, what brings you the most joy? What energizes you the most? Alternatively, what depletes your energy?
3. What are some of your own professional goals, and how can I help you achieve them? Where do you see yourself in five years? These goals could be here or at another impactful organization, but I'd love to know what you're thinking—so that I can help get you there.
4. How can I expand my support for you in this role? What are some of the ways I can increase support for the tools you need to thrive? Are there things I might shift in your responsibilities that may energize you and help you thrive?

Show Your Humanity

Finally, in your leadership role, it's important to show a bit of vulnerability and "just be a human." Often leaders feel they need to have a certain persona inside the office, leaving all other parts of their personality off campus. I disagree. Your teams want and deserve authenticity. It's also a lot less stressful to lead when you bring your authentic self to the table. Satyajit Dattagupta at Northeastern University agrees. In an interview, he told me, "Laughter and good humor goes a long way at work. Strong leaders bring out the best in their people. They bring joy to work, they make people laugh. Work should be joyful, but that tone starts at the top."[27]

It's also important to show the utmost humanity to the members of your team. Although enrolling a class is important, nothing is more critical than ensuring your team feels supported when they need to step away from the work. Whether I was serving as a dean or a CEO, I had employees who needed to deal with difficult and often traumatic situations in their own personal lives. I always made sure to show humanity first and allow the staff member to take all the time they need to handle the situation. It's the right thing to do; it also creates an incredible amount of trust in and loyalty to the organization. Even though a short-term absence by one of your staff members may cause a slight inconvenience to you and your team, you must take the long view. I've been fortunate in my career to work for people who led with their hearts and were deeply empathetic during difficult moments in my life. I was allowed to take extended time when my mother passed, when I had to have medical surgery, or when I had to care for a loved one. I've made it a life goal to pay that kindness forward. However, you'd be shocked at the stories I hear from admission officers who were not extended the same grace. It's important to support your staff members in their most difficult hour—to acknowledge their humanity, which, in turn, shines a light on yours.

All this plays into the type of work culture you build for your team. I engage with hundreds of professionals in admission offices today, and what I often hear is that the main reason they are frustrated is not because the job is hard work—it's because they are exhausted from working in toxic cultures. Admission officers have shared that they are denied professional development opportunities or they work for weeks at a time without a day off. They also share that many of their supervisors are micromanagers who don't trust them. The management expert Peter Drucker reminds us that "culture will eat strategy for breakfast," and I have experienced this many times.[28] As a leader, you can have the perfect plan to execute your strategy, but if you have a deteriorating office culture, it will not succeed. Often leaders are so focused on their own goals they lose sight of how culture is evolving in their offices. In fact, one of the most important things you must do as you transition into a new role is try to understand the culture you are inheriting and then assess whether it's something that needs to evolve. In his book *The First 90 Days*, Michael Watkins writes, "Because cultural habits and norms operate powerfully to reinforce the status quo, it is vital to diagnose problems in the existing culture and to figure out how to begin to address them."[29] A culture that lacks trust, respect, and psychological safety will produce negative outcomes. I know, because I saw it with my own eyes.

In June of 2015, I arrived at Trinity College in Connecticut as the new vice president for enrollment and student success. On my first day, I realized something was amiss with the office culture. Most staff members would come in and not say, "Good morning" to each other. They would immediately walk to their offices and close the door. During my first few days, I held individual meetings to get to know the team. I realized then that most of the staff didn't like each other. Most people had an axe to grind with their colleagues. There was a feeling that some colleagues had better deals than others did. (Some were allowed to work from home a few days a week while others were not, etc.) They didn't trust each other, and they didn't trust the institution. I immediately wondered how these people get anything done together. How do they put on a smile for the students and families they serve every day, when they barely smile at work? Most important, why would they want to come to work at a place with no joy?

At that moment, I realized that, until I helped cultivate a new culture, nothing I tried to implement would succeed. I knew that culture change had to start at the top and immediately began building and cultivating my leadership team. As Disney CEO Bob Iger notes, "When the people at the top of a company have a dysfunctional relationship, there's no way that the rest of the company can be functional."[30] Culture change is hard work. It takes an extraordinary amount of time, energy, emotion, strategy, and consistency. You will lose some staff members during the process, but you will attract and retain those that are eager for positive change. You will slowly gain their trust, which in my experience is the most important ingredient of a positive culture. As organizational consultant and executive coach Jennifer Desjarlais constantly reminds me, "culture is built at the speed of trust."[31]

Each of my leadership roles has required significant culture change management. Although each situation was different, a key strategy for success in each was agreeing on a set of staff mission and values. This can be a strong first step in building a solid organizational culture.

Although institutions have their own mission statements, a staff mission and values statement speaks to the work that you do in your division every day. A mission statement should speak to what your team does and what it represents, whereas values are a list of guiding principles that you all agree to adhere to in the workplace.[32] When I've led mission and values exercises, I usually bring the team together at an offsite retreat, where they can think creatively and not be distracted by the tasks of a typical workday.

In the case of NACAC, we grappled with the question, What does it mean to come to work at NACAC? What do we believe in, what do we stand for, and whom do we serve? We also grappled with the question, What are the values we want to hold each other accountable for in the workplace? As staff members, how do we want to show up, and what are the values we feel are most important in helping us do our best work?

It's important to divide teams into small groups to discuss these questions. Discussing them in large groups does not allow all voices to be heard. We usually spend an entire day engaging in multiple exercises and arrive at a list of possibilities for both a mission statement and values. I then ask for a group of small volunteers to form a committee that will make a final recommendation to the leadership team and staff. In my experience, the staff is usually delighted by the final product, given that they helped create it.

Once the new mission and values have been adopted, they must not disappear into a document that lives on a shelf. One of the things to consider is how you

Examples of Staff Mission and Values Statements

- **NACAC staff mission:** We are the stewards of, and trusted source for, our diverse membership and the students they champion.[33]
- **NACAC staff values:** We embrace collaboration, inclusivity, integrity, compassion, respect, and innovation.
- **Trinity College Division of Enrollment and Student Success staff mission:** We enroll and cultivate intellectually engaged students and prepare them to lead transformative lives.
- **Trinity College Division of Enrollment and Student Success staff values:** We are thoughtful in our work, we listen first, it is ok to ask for help, we are trusted, we always assume best intentions, we admit our mistakes, we don't judge, we present solutions not just problems, we approach our work with optimism, we speak with one voice.

and your team will hold each other accountable for the values you chose. It's important to have the mission statement and values in visible places in your office. In every organization I've worked in, I've had the staff mission and values framed and gifted to the staff. Most of them display these on their desks. I've also had the mission and vision painted on the walls in the office—a live reminder of our shared sense of purpose.

When a new employee starts at NACAC, the mission and values are written on their salary letter. They are also written in the first chapter of the employee handbook. We incorporate the values into annual evaluations, and we celebrate our team members when they exhibit them. We have a wall in our office where people post sticky-note "shout outs" to team members who have gone above and beyond in living our values, and a virtual version exists on Microsoft Teams. Our NACAC office walls are covered with photos of our members at our conferences and events and students who roam the halls of the college fairs we host around the globe. These symbols are incredibly important. They are a daily reminder of our "why." Your office and physical space must represent your mission, your values, and your why.

I also start every meeting with "mission moments." Before we talk about the budget, operations, or challenges of the day, I ask my team to reflect on what is happening across the organization that reminds us of our mission. It's an opportunity to celebrate our wins—big or small. It's a reminder of our purpose and reason for working at NACAC. It keeps our spirits lifted during difficult moments, and it allows us to reflect on how we impact the community we serve.

Finally, it's important to recognize that culture evolves over time, and it can easily shift—so your job as the leader is to keep an active pulse on culture. Every few years, I bring the entire staff together and ask if the staff mission and values are still relevant. If they need updating, the team does it together. Also, my leadership team and my assistant help me keep a pulse on the organization and always inform me when they feel something is impacting the culture. I make sure to address those issues immediately, before they become larger. I also try to have a direct and open line of communication with all of my employees. I have an open-door policy, and I also host CEO office hours—a time when any employee can come in to talk to me about whatever is on their mind. You'd be amazed what people are willing to share and how much you will learn about your office culture just by opening your door and inviting your staff into a conversation.

The Power of Your Assistant

In every leadership role I've held, I've made it my number one priority to develop a strong and trusting relationship with my assistant. They have been my eyes and ears and have helped me keep a pulse on anything I might need to address in the office. I encourage them to be honest with me and to help me keep a pulse on office culture. The minute anything goes awry, they immediately let me know so that I can address it. Consider your assistant your most important partner in this work. When it comes to issues around culture, you should address them immediately. Anything you avoid now can become a culture barrier later.

Advice from the Deans

On Building Your Team

Every dean I interviewed for this project emphasized the importance of hiring well and putting energy into cultivating your teams. They all felt strongly that hiring a diverse team who can help them think differently and solve problems creatively is the key to succeeding in these complex roles.

> Hiring a strong team is critical, and so is your setting of expectations. I am always very clear with my team. This is where we are going, and why. If you decide to get on this train, we are not getting off until it pulls into the station on May 1st.
>
> —Satyajit Dattagupta, executive vice chancellor, chief enrollment officer, and senior advisor to the president, Northeastern University[34]

> You do not do this work alone. Hire people that are going to compliment you. This doesn't mean that they think and work like you. It means exactly the opposite. They bring different ways of operating to the table.

That's how you will best solve problems. That's how you will exceed your goals.

—Adele C. Brumfield, vice provost for enrollment management, University of Michigan[35]

Hiring people who are smarter than you requires "informed vulnerability." Where you have an objective—ideally formally assessed—list of your strengths and weaknesses, be it through something like a Kolbe test or Clifton StrengthsFinder. It's easier—and quicker—for you to hire people with the skills that complement yours. Think about the team's skills and experiences, and where you fit within that array.

—Ken Anselment, former vice president for enrollment and communication, Lawrence University[36]

When you move from director to dean, there is a temptation to jump in and solve all of the problems. Hopefully, you have a good team to do that for you. Ask yourself, what are the things that I should be worried about, and what are the things that I uniquely can solve? Let the good people you've hired shine by handling the rest.

—Satyajit Dattagupta, executive vice chancellor, chief enrollment officer, and senior advisor to the president, Northeastern University[37]

Hire a team who inspires you, and who will push you. They should be your thought partners, and they should also challenge you.

—Whitney Soule, vice provost, dean of admissions, University of Pennsylvania[38]

When you hire people, you have a tremendous responsibility to serve them well. Your job is to cultivate them, to invest in them and to set up an environment where they are able to thrive. That is your number one responsibility, and it will pay dividends for years to come.

—Mark Steinlage, vice president for enrollment management, Rockhurst University[39]

CHAPTER 3

The Power of Storytelling

Admission officers are powerful storytellers. It's a requirement of the job. As an admission counselor, you are trained to paint a picture of what life can be like on your campus and teach students how to navigate the admission process at your institution. Through high school visits, information sessions, college fairs, parent nights, and more, you deliver speeches with the aim of getting students excited about your institution. As you grow in the field, you may oversee marketing or communications within the admission office. You learn how to create compelling stories through social media, printed marketing materials, or websites that help your audience learn as much as they can.

In my experience, these important skills are the foundation of the deanship. In many ways, those who "grow up" in the college admission counseling profession have an advantage when they become leaders because they bring a rich history of storytelling to their roles. Yet something significantly changes when you reach the deanship, and you will be required to approach your work differently. You are now one of the chief storytellers of the institution. Your storytelling is no longer just geared toward prospective students, families, and counselors—your constituency expands exponentially. As the leader of a critical area of the institution, you must now work to keep students, faculty, staff, trustees, the president, and sometimes even your legislators informed. Given the enrollment challenges many institutions face today, admission deans are often charged with change management in what has historically been a very slow-moving sector.

This is why mastering the art of storytelling is critical for success. According to Frances X. Frei and Anne Morriss in *The Harvard Business Review*, "Storytelling is the essential human activity. The harder the situation, the more essential it is. When your organization needs to make a big change, stories will help you convey why it needs to transform but also what the future will look like in specific, vivid terms."[1]

Your job as a dean is to inspire the community toward a vision. Impactful deans don't just bring in a class—they inspire a community around shared values and a hope for what the campus community could be. You get to determine what story you will tell about the institution to external audiences, but even more important, you get to create the internal narrative that's critical to your success.

Impactful deans also become champions for a cause. For example, many deans today are champions for financial aid, helping their trustees, alumni, and other constituents understand the urgency of raising more funds for financial aid and increasing access for students who can't afford to pay full tuition. This requires strategic storytelling. It also requires you to step out of your day-to-day role of dean (enrolling a class) and fighting for issues that will make the campus stronger. I did this when I was at Pitzer College by moving the institution toward admitting more international students, giving them financial aid, and expanding access for Deferred Action for Childhood Arrivals (DACA) students in California. At Trinity, I traveled with the president to make the case to alumni and trustees that we needed more financial aid for middle- and low-income families and more resources to ensure that, once students enrolled, we created the support systems they needed to succeed.

These initiatives required an incredible amount of compelling storytelling and dot-connecting. Further, I had to be willing to step out of my day-to-day role and become a champion for the cause. When you take on the deanship, you too will become the champion for several issues that impact the entire institution.

In this chapter, I first present a set of actionable storytelling strategies and considerations, from reminding the community of your priorities to leveraging data, connecting the dots, and always celebrating wins. I will then shift my focus to five broader principles of effective storytelling: maintaining transparency, contextualizing the narrative, incorporating external voices, providing a roadmap, and utilizing symbols. We'll end with tips for improving your storytelling skills and "Advice from the Deans."

STORYTELLING STRATEGIES

Remind the Community of Your Charge

Often, institutions go through extensive searches to hire a new dean. They spend months putting together position profiles, which usually outline the goals for the position. Once the new dean is hired, those position profiles sit on shelves, and most people forget what the specific calls to action were. Unless, however, you are Lee Coffin, vice president and dean of admission and financial aid at Dartmouth College. When he first arrived at Dartmouth, he would take his position profile with him to various stakeholder meetings and continued to do so throughout his tenure in the role. He used it as a reminder to the community of what his charge was. When he proposed changes or innovations, he would remind constituents that this wasn't a goal he created—rather, it was one the community created together.[2] It's critical to constantly remind the community of what you were hired to do, and even more important, why.

In my deanships, I often would do something similar with strategic plans. At both institutions I served, I would examine the goals of the strategic plan and use them to create related stories around some of the initiatives my office was working on. This reminded the community of where we were going and how the dean of admission was contributing to the vision set forth by the institution.

It's All About Trade-Offs

In today's challenging higher education landscape, institutions are not going to be able to get everything they want, and it's going to be your job to remind them of that. In every institution where I served as dean, faculty wanted the best and brightest students, the president wanted the most diverse classes, the CFO wanted more revenue, trustees wanted stronger average test scores, each academic department wanted students interested in their academic areas, coaches wanted the most competitive athletes—the list goes on. Ken Anselment still recalls this challenge during his years as vice president for enrollment and communication at Lawrence University. "It's our classic conundrum: if we're doing our jobs most effectively, we are not going to make everyone happy. When you learn to live with this as an enrollment leader—and sooner is best—you will be able to weather the storm clouds that gather (and they will gather) in the wake of the decisions you get to make."[3]

Your job as a dean is to help the community understand that when you can't have it all, you have to make difficult decisions about what you aren't willing to compromise on and what sacrifices you are willing to make. Zakiya Smith Ellis, former secretary of higher education in New Jersey, reflected on advice from former President Barack Obama when she served as senior advisor for education on the White House domestic policy council. "President Obama used to remind us that all of the decisions at an executive level involve some kind of trade-off," she says. "If there is ever something that is just rainbows and bunnies and unicorns and wonderful, someone has already done it; it's taken. The only thing you are dealing with (at the executive level) are trade-offs—and difficult trade-offs."[4]

Transparency Is Key: Share the Good and the Bad

It's tempting to only share good news with your community, but if you are going to mobilize them toward change, you must share the bad. Transparency is critical. If your institution has missed enrollment targets for years and has been losing students in its inquiry pool, it's important to share that. However, it's important to share this not from an alarmist perspective but rather as a piece of information that will light a fire under people. In every crisis lies opportunity. According to Kotter, the first rule of organizational change is to create a sense of urgency.[5] You can create a sense of urgency through storytelling—by being transparent about what the challenge is, what you hope to see on the other side, and what help you are going to need from the community to get you there. Jennifer Desjarlais believes that storytelling is an important tool for persuasion. She notes, "Storytelling is part of the process of persuasion; it helps critical constituents imagine, understand and identify what is possible. The role of leadership then is to help to clarify the concern, identify what is at stake, what is needed and how it might be engaged."[6]

At both institutions where I served as Dean, I had a practice that helped me create a sense of urgency for the trustees around fundraising for financial aid. Every few years, I would put up a slide with data about all of the students we did not admit to the college. I would then show them what the academic profile and demographics were for those students. I would also highlight the personal stories and exceptional achievements of some of those students I did not admit. The trustees were often stunned, and until some of them caught onto my strategy, I could tell some were visibly angry. "How could you possibly not admit these students? They are incredible!" they would remark. My response was always the same. "I didn't have enough financial aid. If I had a stronger budget, these are the kinds of students we could have on our campus." I would then ask for their support in raising funds for financial aid and for making it a top priority in the institution's strategy.

Increasing college access for low-income and first-generation students from all over the globe has always been the cause I've championed on campuses. I have seen many deans of admission mobilize their own communities around their causes. They've done so by telling stories about what the challenges are, showing the community what the trade-offs are, and asking for their help in bringing forth change. These deans led with transparency, but instead of just sounding an alarm, they made the alarm a call to action. Transparency and storytelling can be a powerful force for change on a campus.

Keep It Simple and Clear

To galvanize your community around a cause, you must make sure they understand the issues. In their *Harvard Business Review* article, Frances X. Frei and Anne Morriss note, "Before you can solve an urgent organizational problem, you need to take a crucial first step: craft a clear, compelling story that harnesses everyone's energy and directs it toward change."[7]

The truth is, academics are infamous for using complex language that most people don't understand, and admission deans are no better. We use terms like *ED, EA, FAFSA, econometric modeling, financial aid optimization, CRM, net tuition revenue*, and *more.* When crafting your storytelling, it's important to keep in mind most of your constituents are not experts in enrollment management. It's important for you to convey the nuances and complexity of enrollment management but do so in simple terms, especially because most of the public assumes your job is pretty simple. In fact, I still remember moving into the dean role at Pitzer College, and a faculty member saying to me, "Your job isn't so hard. You just need to go to a few more high schools and get a few more students." That same year, a trustee who worked for a major airline told me, "I could do your job with my eyes shut. In the airline industry, we can always predict how many people will show up for a flight. It's the same thing as your student yield predictions." In both instances, I smiled with grace and realized I had my storytelling work cut out for me.

Data Is Critical

Data is absolutely critical to your success. When you are telling your stories, data visualization can be a very powerful tool. Author Brené Brown reminds us that "stories are just data with soul."[8] You will want to show data to convince the community of the urgency of the matter. However, it is critical that you don't just stop at the data. You must remind the community that behind the data are students, real young people whose lives are transformed through the work that you all do on your campus. In my experience, so many of my campus constituents were obsessed with making sure our data "looked good." My job was to remind them the data had real consequences for the lives of our students and the health of our institution. I was adamant about reminding the community that, although it's easy to succumb to the pressures of rankings and other data points that make campus leaders feel good, it's important to allow data to inform us (to be data informed) not to be the sole reason we make certain decisions (to be data driven). The distinction is key.

In the college admission profession, Jon Boeckenstedt of Oregon State University is best known for his use of data to tell stories. In fact, he publishes a well-known blog that is often quoted in higher education media. He has always been passionate about using data to tell stories and mobilize communities. He shared an example of his impact with me:

> I worked at DePaul for 17 years; if you know anything about DePaul, it might be that its original image was as a commuter school for students from the city of Chicago. But in the 1980s and 1990s, both the Loop and the Lincoln Park areas of Chicago underwent dramatic changes; both became far more attractive to students from beyond the city, and the image of Chicago itself became a factor in the university's image.
>
> But cultural change is very hard, and many of the people in the communications office, alumni office, and even admissions had a hard time talking to people who were not already in the city. I sensed there was the potential for us to do better in distant markets, and I used NCES/IPEDS data to frame the challenge and the opportunity. Not many people know that every other year, colleges are required to report the geographic makeup of their first-year student classes, but that information can provide a lot of insight into your market and your market opportunities.

> I showed how constrained our footprint was compared to our main competitors, and showed what states provided most of their geographic diversity, and identified a few areas where investment in marketing and recruitment could pay big dividends. And I talked to our people about how these markets were different and had different motivations in choosing a college. We added new regional recruitment staff in parts of the country, and it paid off in less than two years.
>
> Data were important and supported the idea, but it was still important to filter that raw information through context and culture for it to make sense to people.[9]

Turning data into stories is a powerful tool to inspire a community toward action. Rajesh Mirchandani, former BBC news correspondent and founder of Storytelling Consulting, reminds us that "there's a reason human beings have gathered around camp fires and dinner tables for thousands of years sharing stories not datapoints. Data appeals to our brains but stories move our hearts."[10]

ABCD

My first several years as NACAC CEO, I walked around the office saying, "ABCD." I also used the term in my board presentation, and now it's become a term the whole team uses. It means: Always Be Connecting Dots. The original concept comes from restaurateur Danny Meyer, who believes that his team should "always be collecting dots" of information.[11] I evolved that concept to connecting dots as often as possible.

Connecting dots is a critical part of storytelling. If you don't tell people why you are doing something, and how it connects to what they care most about, you will have an uphill battle every time you try to make a change or implement something new.

Institutions of higher education deal with constant change. For example, every year, new faculty arrive. Students graduate and others enroll. You have new board members, trustees, and so on. This is why, regardless of how often you've told a story or explained why you are doing something, you continually have to help the community connect the dots. Sometimes my own staff members would notice that my communications to the community included details I'd shared in the past. "You already told them this," some would remark. "I know," I would say. "And we have to tell them again and again until the story really sticks." It's better to overinform than to underinform.

Every year, whether I was presenting to the student government, trustees, or the faculty—I would assume there were people in the room who knew nothing about enrollment issues and goals of the past. I would start from scratch. Here are our challenges. Here is how those challenges compare to the national landscape. Here is where we've been, here is our progress, here is where we are going, here is why.

Each time something happened that was related to our work or goals, I would connect the dots. If a faculty member wrote me to thank me for the incredible students they find a joy to teach, I would share that note with my staff and connect the dots to the incredible work they have been doing. When we would enroll more low-income students with incredible life stories, personal, and academic achievements, I would share those stories with trustees, donors, and those that made significant investments to increase our financial aid resources. I wanted them to see how their commitments made the college stronger and how their investments were changing lives.

Lee Coffin at Dartmouth does this with the board of trustees. As he gives them updates about changes or progress, he points back to the position profile that was created for his role. He reminds the board about the charge he was given and connects the dots to how his current work is a direct response to his charge.[12]

At NACAC, I spend a lot of time connecting dots. With more than twenty-eight thousand members, twenty-three affiliate organizations, a twenty-member board, and a new board chair elected each year, storytelling is critical to ensuring the organization stays the course. Every year, as we onboard new leaders into the organization, we start from scratch. Even though I know there are many who know and understand the challenges and successes the organization has had since my arrival, I always start from the beginning. I want everyone to understand why it is we make the decisions we make. I want all of our constituents to know that everything we do is intentional, has an origin story, and connects to a larger goal or mission of the association. In my opinion, you can never tell too many stories.

I also deliver a "state of the association" address at our national conference most years. This is the biggest dot-connector of the year. I share successes and challenges we have faced, and I remind the membership of where the organization has been, and where we are going. When we have success, I immediately connect the dots to the people, groups, or individuals who've made it possible. And I always end with a note about where we are going.

Finally, it's important not to personalize goals. When you arrive at an institution, you are there to deliver on a goal that has been set by the president, board, and so on. You must constantly remind the community of this by connecting the dots. After a while, you become a part of the fabric of the institution, and it's natural that people begin to personalize things. During my time in higher education, some people accused me of only wanting to admit more low-income students because it represented my own background. I reminded the community that, although this was certainly true about my lived experience (and yes, I am very passionate about this cause), I was at the institution to deliver on a goal that was set by the community. Again, remember Lee Coffin's strategy? Although you don't have to do it his way, you need to find your own. Every opportunity you get, connect the dots.

Celebrate

Celebrations are also part of storytelling and connecting the dots. I feel strongly that when you achieve success, you celebrate. According to Jamil Zaki in *The Harvard Business Review*, "One way to lock in a sense of efficacy and will is to pay close attention to progress and celebrate it. Focusing people on their wins, and how they have managed to take control of their work lives, makes them more likely to feel agency in the future."[13]

It's great for the morale of your team, and it also helps other members of your organization see progress. When I was an admission dean, every year, I would host a celebration in May—to toast the new students that would enroll at the institution. I would invite anyone on campus that was involved in the recruitment of the class. The admission and financial aid teams, coaches, faculty who volunteered for open houses and other programs, tour guides, etc. It takes a village to enroll a class, and that village should celebrate.

The celebration was a reminder of the goals we had set—and whether we met, exceeded, or missed the goal slightly, we would celebrate. This was my way of helping the community connect the dots. It told a story of collaboration: we are all responsible for enrollment success, not just the admission office. It also was a great morale booster for my staff. So often admission teams work so hard for an entire year under very challenging circumstances. They enroll the class and move on to the next one. It's important to pause and celebrate—it's a reminder that there is joy in this work. In fact, Ken Anselment shares that "at Lawrence University, we

Celebrate, Regardless of the Outcome

In today's challenging enrollment landscape, many institutions will miss their enrollment targets. Don't make the mistake of not celebrating the hard work of your teams. Whether you made your goal or not, your teams have worked hard to enroll the first-year and transfer students who will be arriving on your campus in the new semester. You must acknowledge that work, or else morale will plummet. Even more important is to involve key stakeholders at the institution to acknowledge the work as well. La Jerne Terry Cornish, president of Ithaca College, feels passionately about this. During a panel discussion at NACAC's annual conference in Los Angeles in 2024, she shared that Ithaca College had missed their enrollment target by a few hundred students. She called the community together, not to be alarmist, but rather to celebrate the many students the admission office had brought in that year. She feels strongly you need to support your enrollment teams, especially in challenging times.[14] I do too. Don't forget to celebrate your teams regardless of the outcome.

would always gather on May 1 as a team to celebrate the work we did together, regardless of the outcome, because it's the quality of the work—and not of the result—that we can control."[15]

Finally, I encourage you to invite your teams into storytelling and celebrating on a regular basis. One way I have done this over the years is by starting every one of my staff meetings with a "mission moment." This is an opportunity for anyone on the team to share something positive that is happening in the organization that represents our mission, values, or goals. Over the years, team members have shared everything from completing a successful event, to balancing the budget, creating something new, or exceeding goals. It is a wonderful reminder that good things are happening all year and that you are collectively moving toward your goals. Starting meetings on a celebratory note also sets the tone for the entire meeting. I've practiced this ritual for many years, and now some of my leadership team members ask their teams to share mission moments on a regular basis. This is an example of how you can create a culture of storytelling and celebration across your entire organization.

PRINCIPLES FOR EFFECTIVE STORYTELLING

1. Maintain Transparency

Transparency has been addressed in other sections of this book, but it's important to continue to mention it in different contexts. It sounds simple, but if you aren't transparent with your community about enrollment issues, you will quickly lose credibility. It's important to share the good news and the bad news. If the community does not understand the challenges and their nuances, they won't know how to support you. I will admit that transparency today takes an incredible amount of courage. A photo of one of your data slides taken at a faculty meeting could quickly end up on social media. It's also never fun to deliver bad news. The backlash can be painful. But a lack of transparency is just not an option. It does not mean you have to share every data point, but you need to be able to share enough where the community knows what's happening, what the challenges are, and how you plan to address them (with their help, of course).

I still remember arriving at Trinity College and attending my first faculty meeting, where I unveiled detailed data about the composition of recent incoming classes and shared some of my own analysis, which included reasons why I believed the institution needed to change its strategy around admission and financial aid. One faculty member walked over to me afterward and said, "Wow, what you just shared isn't pretty, but I'm so grateful. No one has ever showed that to us. Clearly we have our work cut out for us, but you have my support." Share the good stories and the challenging ones too. When you lead through transparency, you will earn trust.

2. Contextualize Your Story

A part of your storytelling on a campus has to be about sharing the national and global context. Higher education does not function in a silo, and it's important for your constituents to understand the ecosystem in which higher education operates. On every campus where I served as dean, I constantly shared articles from *The Chronicle of Higher Education*, *Inside Higher Ed*, *Ed Dive*, *Education Week*, and other education and mainstream media outlets to help colleagues understand what was happening in higher education across the nation and how it related to our campus.

Each year, I would share data about demographics, so they understood the decline in students in certain parts of the country and how our recruitment goals were getting more challenging each year. I would share Western Interstate Commission for Higher Education (WICHE) data, National Student Clearinghouse Data, Open Doors Data, as well as data about emerging economies around the globe where we might consider expanding our recruitment efforts. I also kept a pulse on what was happening around the globe and tried to keep my community abreast of global trends. Because your constituents don't always understand the broader context of stories in the higher education media, your role also puts you in the position of chief translator in your community. Help your campus understand what stories should matter to them, as well as those that shouldn't.

I still remember presenting at a board of trustees meeting in January 2020. I warned the board there was a pandemic that had spread in China. I predicted we would have a hard time enrolling students from China that year, which could have a significant impact on our budget. Little did I know this would become a global pandemic bringing extraordinary challenge and change to our institutions and our world. It's critical to share context with your community. In ensures they understand the challenges you and your team are up against, but it also helps to mobilize them around your cause. On every campus I've served, the community was used to me reminding them everyone was responsible for our enrollment success, not just the admission office.

3. Incorporate External Voices

Although your role is to become one of the institution's chief storytellers, it's also important to incorporate outside voices to validate and emphasize the important messages you feel your community should be aware of. Many deans of admission invite national experts to speak to their boards of trustees, cabinets, alumni groups, or faculty. I was no different. At each institution where I served as admission dean, I would invite outside speakers to share their experiences with enrollment, to discuss demographic trends, or flag national issues that could impact the admission goals of the institution. Depending on the audience, I would invite a different expert to help inform my community. Sometimes, I would invite scholars who are doing work on enrollment issues (such as Nathan Grawe from Carleton College, whose book on demographic trends does a phenomenal job of explaining the demographic cliff).[16] Other times, I would invite high school counselors who work directly with students to help the community understand the pressures students are facing in the admission pipeline. Often, I would invite consultants who work at a variety of higher education institutions by helping them with enrollment goals—such as EAB or RHB. These firms had a wealth of data that highlighted the enrollment trends and challenges across the country. The data was powerful storytelling that my community needed to hear.

Now that I serve as NACAC CEO, I often travel to campuses to meet with cabinets and boards to discuss national trends and brainstorm how to prepare for the enrollment challenges that lie ahead. What I find interesting is that every dean or president who invites me to speak has told their constituents the same message I deliver. Yet, the community is usually moved toward action because an "outside expert" has given them advice. If you're looking to create a stronger sense of urgency on your campus, you may want to invite an outside storyteller to support you.

4. Provide a Roadmap

To mobilize a community toward a cause, you must constantly remind them of where you're all going, together. Just like institutions of higher education have strategic plans and they measure progress along the way, admission deans need to do the same. Every opportunity you get, remind your constituents of what the goals are and connect the dots to how they will contribute to those goals. Lee Coffin at Dartmouth says, "Your job is to translate over and over and over again to all of your constituents—where are we, where are we going, and why are we going there?"[17]

When I was on campus, I would remind faculty, staff, students, trustees, and others about our enrollment goals, our revenue goals, our academic quality goals, and more. Each time we made progress on a goal, I would share it. These kind of updates generate excitement, uplift the community, and remind them that they have a role to play.

At NACAC, I do the same. At every board of directors meeting, I provide a CEO update. During this update, I share progress and challenges. At the end of each presentation, I show the board the same slide I've shown them since I became CEO. It is a slide of what we believe NACAC should achieve by 2030. During the question-and-answer period, I leave the slide up and visible to the group because I want to make sure they know where we are headed. I do the same for other various NACAC leadership groups I present to and for our staff.

5. Utilize Symbols

In his book, *Start with Why*, author Simon Sinek writes it's important to use symbols in storytelling. He reminds us of how Martin L. King Jr. chose to give his speech at the Lincoln Memorial as a symbol of an American value: freedom for all. He also reminds us that Ronald Reagan also used symbols throughout his storytelling: "Ronald Reagan, the great communicator, knew all too well the power of symbols. In 1982, he was the first president to invite a 'hero' to sit in the balcony of the House chamber during the State of the Union address, a tradition that has continued every year since. A man who exuded optimism, Reagan knew the value of symbolizing the values of America instead of just talking about them."[18]

At a college, there is no greater symbol than your students. It's important to use their stories—their triumphs, successes, and challenges to help bring to life the data you are sharing with your constituents—or to make the cause for change.

I still remember the day I used this strategy with the Trinity College board of trustees. The year after I moved the college toward a test-optional policy, some members of the community were still skeptical about the change. Some weren't sure if the students we were admitting were "high quality," or if the policy change was going to impact the academic preparation and rigor of the incoming students.

During a board meeting, I invited a large group of students (if I remember correctly, I invited about ten) to be on a panel. I moderated and asked each of them to tell their stories. Where were they from, how did they find out about the college, and what had their transition been like? It was a diverse set of students from all over the country and the world. One by one, they awed the trustees with their wit, passion for academics, and co-curricular activities. The trustees were also impressed by their geographic diversity. Several of the students were not from regions where Trinity tended to attract students. Toward the end of the panel, instead of asking the final question of a student, I asked it of the board. "What do all of these students have in common?" They guessed several things, but none got the answer correct. "None of these students submitted test scores in their admission process."

"You mean, we would've missed out on these amazing students if we still required the test," one board member clarified. Then, many of the students chimed

Leverage Your Mission Statement as a Symbol

Once you have a mission statement for your division (discussed in chapter 2), put it on the walls and make it highly visible. Make sure the mission of the institution is visible, as well. Have photos of students and images of success stories on your walls. If your team has won awards, proudly display them. When people walk into your building, you want there to be no guessing about what you do, what you aspire to, and what some of your successes have been. I visit many admission offices across the country, and the symbols I find are extraordinary—student success videos in the lobby, music from student acapella groups playing in the background, posters congratulating students and alumni on Fulbright awards and other fellowships, notifications about the millions of dollars disbursed in financial aid, or the types of jobs and graduate programs students are headed to after commencement. The types of uplifting symbols you can share are endless. Don't take this storytelling strategy lightly. It will inspire your community and prospective students.

in and confirmed that, yes, part of the reason they applied was because the college didn't require testing and was interested much more in their backgrounds and interests than just the test.

This approach was incredibly effective in promoting this initiative with the board of trustees. Storytelling is a powerful tool and is even more powerful when you can use the symbols you have on your campus to deliver the story.

Finally, it's important to recognize that in today's challenging admission landscape, it is easy for the community to forget the higher purpose of enrolling a class. It's your job to remind the community that the students who enroll at your institution become the institution, and therefore your admission policies and practices must be managed with great care. At every institution where I served as admission dean, I would remind the community that my job was to operationalize the mission and vision of the organization. I did that through the strategic enrollment and stewardship of students and their experience. Although I was the architect of the work, everyone in the community had a role to play in our success.

Improve Your Storytelling

There are various tactics you can use to strengthen your own storytelling on campus. A few of the following tips (adapted from "Vision to Victory: The Art of Storytelling," from *Maven*[19]) help you structure your arguments and ensure that your audiences feel inspired by your call to action.

1. Structure

It may feel reminiscent of our English 101 first-year courses, but a compelling story must have a beginning, middle, and end. It should have a powerful opening that captures your audience, robust information throughout that helps your audience understand the context, and a climax or call to action at the end. The best stories use a clear structure to elicit an emotion or reaction from listeners; in the context of your admission deanship, your stories should probably also have a call to action.

2. Relatability

Your stories have to differ, depending on the audience. Although your end goal may be the same, each audience has to feel like it can relate to your story. How you explain your strategy to an alumni body is not the same way you would offer it to faculty members. Always ask yourself, what does this audience care about? Through what lens do they view this issue? The story has to be relatable and told in a style and context they can understand.

3. Emotional Appeal

Successful stories elicit emotions. This is why it's important to personalize each story, to connect to your audience in ways that will resonate. Remember that regardless of the politics at your institution, there are two things every constituent has in common: They care deeply for the institution, and they care deeply for students. Rajesh Mirchandani says that "as a leader, storytelling with vulnerability gives people a window into your world and your challenges. It allows them to see their role in co-creating solutions."[20] Create emotional appeal based on shared passions, and your stories will always resonate.

4. Clarity and Brevity

Academics are not known for brevity, and deans of admission aren't either. We often give too much detail, and it can take away from the impact of our story. Effective storytelling is clear and brief. Stories that are long and complex can also sound defensive. In my experience, it's always better for you to tell the story as concisely and clearly as possible, with passion, and a call to action. Then you allow your audience to ask you questions, where the rest of the details can be filled.

5. Conflict and Resolution

Conflict and resolution are both crucial to good storytelling. As you build your narrative, share what the problem is and how it was created. Then share how the challenge can be overcome and how your audience can help you achieve this. Your call to action should always be optimistic and include a vision for the road ahead.

Advice from the Deans

On Storytelling

Every dean I interviewed considered themselves one of the institution's chief storytellers. They all felt strongly that you must personalize every narrative and remind the community of where you are going, and most important, why it matters.

> Storytelling provides the clarity and cohesion required to deliver a compelling narrative with powerful points that maintain the focus on critical areas in the midst of internal and external pressures, ongoing change and transition.
>
> —Jennifer Desjarlais, former dean of admission and financial aid, Wellesley College and principal, Cambridge Hill Partners Inc.[21]

One of the most powerful stories you can tell on campus is your own. Most of us come to this work for deeply personal reasons, including having a transformative undergraduate experience. Share those stories. It helps people understand why you are doing the work, why you are fighting for this cause.

—Kasey Urquidez, former vice president, enrollment management, and dean, admissions, University of Arizona[22]

The way you sell an idea to your community is to tell stories. You start with why, then you create a compelling vision, and help people understand what the strategy is to get there. You can't mobilize people around a cause without these three components.

—Mark Steinlage, vice president for enrollment management, Rockhurst University[23]

Data is critical for storytelling. In aggregate, enrollment data are interesting, but it's only when they're broken apart that they become compelling. Unless you work for an institution that has an abundance of resources, it's likely that every decision made involves some trade-offs, and in some sense, the most important job for enrollment professionals (whether in admissions, financial aid, retention, or other areas) is to help people understand those trade-offs: When you pull a string here, this is where and how things unravel. Setting reasonable expectations about competing priorities helps people understand and participate in enrollment decisions and avoids the tendency of universities to approach strategy the way a four-year-old approaches Christmas.

—Jon Boeckenstedt, vice provost of enrollment management, Oregon State University[24]

Over time, you will realize that admissions deans are required to engage in storytelling almost every day on the job. Sometimes, it will be in formal ways—like presenting to the faculty or trustees. Other days it will be less formal, like helping your staff understand why a decision was made. Regardless of your audience, the storytelling requires careful preparation and maneuvering. Don't go into situations unprepared. Always ask yourself, what do I really want to say, what do I want my audience to feel, and how do I want this moment to be remembered?

—Whitney Soule, vice provost and dean of admission, University of Pennsylvania[25]

CHAPTER 4

Becoming an Astute Politician

On university campuses, everything is political, and all politics are local.
—Adele C. Brumfield, vice provost for enrollment management, University of Michigan

In higher education, there are the written rules, and then there are the hidden nuances of each campus you must learn to maneuver. One of the biggest surprises I encountered when I first became a dean was how political the job is. College campuses are steeped in politics, and if you don't learn how to strategically navigate them, you won't succeed. I was in awe of how much politicking I had to do to get a policy implemented, a program eliminated, or a new initiative passed.

I quickly learned that, even though I was the leader of a division, it did not mean I always "owned" the final decision in those departments. The number of stakeholders I had to consult before making changes was more than I could have imagined, and as a new dean, I quickly learned that the only "real" power I had was persuasion. If I made big changes without consulting others, I could easily have a faculty protest on my hands, become the feature story in the student newspaper—or worse—the alumni and parent Facebook pages.

When I arrived on campus, I heard a lot of the typical warnings—like "You should know this faculty member has an axe to grind," or "This alumni group really cares about this program, so before you make any changes you make you should consult them." Then there were the things I learned only through experience—like, be careful what car you drive or what clothes you wear. In an age where the common narrative on campus is that administrators are overpaid, everyone watches campus leaders carefully. When I worked at Pitzer College in Claremont, California, I drove a Toyota Prius. A major focus of the school's curriculum and core values was environmental sustainability. If I showed up on campus with an SUV, my commitment to the school would surely be questioned, and the students would certainly have a reason to write about me in their newspaper.

At Pitzer, I still remember sitting in a meeting with a group of faculty members. In the middle of the meeting, a faculty member looked down at my shoes and said, "Must be nice to walk around with designer shoes." I was dumbfounded and didn't know how to react. You could cut the tension in the room with a knife, so I chose to ignore the question and continued with the issues at hand.

In that situation, the faculty member took a personal jab at me at a time when tensions between the administration and faculty were high. The faculty wanted higher wages and were questioning the high salaries of administrators. I'm not saying their approach was fair, and it certainly wasn't kind—but it wasn't the first time something like this happened to me on a campus, and it certainly wasn't the last. Another time, students at Trinity College wrote a story in the campus newspaper about my salary. Once, a faculty member saw me getting into my Volvo station wagon at Trinity College and commented, "It's clear the college is compensating you very well." All of these experiences taught me a great lesson. Be careful what you drive, and be aware of the messages sent, however unintended, by the way you present yourself on campus. People are always watching and listening.

As you transition to a new deanship, part of navigating the politics is understanding the culture of the institution and making sure your actions, behaviors, and yes—even your wardrobe—are a good match. A former dean of admission at an institution in the northeast arrived at her new institution from California. On her first day on the job, some of the staff decided to give her advice on places she could go food shopping in the area. It was a kind gesture, but her response led to a very difficult start for her. "Oh, it's ok, I only shop at Whole Foods," she told her team (a supermarket known for pricier, organic foods). It was an off-the-cuff remark that she did not say to sound pompous. She had some health challenges and could only find some of the products she needed at Whole Foods. Her staff didn't know that, however, and her comment made them feel like she wasn't down to earth. It set the tone for her entire tenure there, and although it wasn't the reason she left a few short years later, the way she presented herself to her team early in her tenure made it difficult to change her reputation.

I do need to acknowledge, however, there is a thin line between navigating politics and being your authentic self. I am a staunch advocate for leaders bringing their authentic selves to their role. My advice is to be aware of the politics and areas of sensitivity on campus and to be aware your actions and choices will reveal things about you to the community (real or imagined). How people respond is beyond your control, but I urge you to be intentional about how you choose to "show up" on campus.

In this chapter, I share strategies for navigating the complex politics of a shared governance system. Each institution has its own history, culture, and informal ways of operating. To succeed in the deanship, you will need to become an astute politician, which I liken to being a campus diplomat. Your job is to inspire people toward a cause, and often you must get them to consensus. How you do that will depend on your ability to understand the power dynamics on campus (formal and informal), cultivate allies, and remain humble.

NAVIGATING SHARED GOVERNANCE

Formal and Informal Networks

In a shared governance model, you work together with many constituents—faculty, administration, governing boards, sometimes students—to make decisions and develop polices. According to the Association of Governing Boards, "Shared governance is one of higher education's most distinctive values and is key to the institutional success of all colleges and universities. It brings stakeholders together around passion for the institution and ensures the inclusion of a range of voices and ideas in the formulation of goals, priorities and strategies. Together, these collaborative voices focus on holistic, strategic directions of the future."[1]

The implications of this system for admission deans are extraordinary. Unlike other sectors, where decisions are made from the top down, in higher education, decisions are made in collaboration with many constituents. Depending on the institution's governance model, a final decision for a policy may rest with the faculty, trustees, president, or state legislature. One of the things a dean must first learn is which decisions are theirs to make and which need consultation, which need a formal vote, and which they should give their constituents a heads up about.

Constituents I Kept Informed

Trustees
President
My staff
Faculty senate chair
Staff council chair
Chair of faculty committee on admission and financial aid
Chair of parents council
Student government president
Alumni board president
Key donors (especially those who funded enrollment initiatives)
Legal counsel

When I was a dean, I created a laminated governance chart. I kept it on my computer, and I also gave a copy to all my direct reports. This chart showed the various levels of governance I had to go through to make a decision. It also illustrated the informal networks I had to consult or inform every time I made a new decision or policy change. It ensured I forgot no one in the process of change and all of my constituents felt included.

As a dean, you will likely need your own customized guide or cheat sheet that reflects your institution's unique governance model. If you comb through the websites of various colleges and universities, you will find many varying definitions of shared governance. This one, from Marshall University in West Virginia, is a good and fairly standard representative:

> Shared governance is a systematized structure of transparent decision-making that reflects shared interests and shared responsibility of all constituent groups. Constituency groups—which include, but are not limited to, faculty, students, staff, the Board of Governors and administration—have assured, protected opportunities to influence decisions regarding the operation and direction of Marshall University and established organizational means by which they can carry these out. The role of constituency groups is not merely advisory; instead, decision-making is actively shared among all groups.[2]

When institutional leaders want to implement change, there are usually formal groups that must be consulted, depending on what the change is—and what constituency it will impact. For example, whether an institution requires standardized testing is not a decision the dean of admission can make alone. Faculty, who have responsibility and oversight of the academic program and curriculum, must be included in the conversation—and depending on the structure of the governance system, often boards of trustees or legislatures (in the case of large state systems) must be involved. In Florida, for example, whether an institution requires testing must be voted upon by the legislature.[3]

Remember, there are formal networks one must navigate and include to follow shared governance models, but there are also informal. At some of the institutions I have served, retired faculty had influence over the current faculty. Some of their opinions were held in very high esteem, and I learned quickly if I wanted certain things to pass in the faculty senate, I needed to include them in my decision-making.

Governance Versus Influencers

A note about local communities: a constituency some admission deans will have to work closely with is local residents and government officials who influence institutional activities. For example, some institutions are restricted in how many students they can enroll because of local legislation. This tends to happen at institutions located in areas that are already overcrowded. But in an age where tuition revenue is critical for institutions to survive, having the local community dictate an enrollment cap can have tremendous implications. American University in Washington, D.C., and University of California, Berkeley, are two of the schools that have been given enrollment caps by their cities.[4] This can create significant tension between the university and the community—and forging relationships with key stakeholders and community influencers will be critical for any dean. An admission dean needs to not only be aware of these issues but also work in collaboration with the local community to ensure the relationship is strong.

Another example of an informal network is the alumni body. Although at many institutions alumni will not get to vote on key policy decisions, they are important stakeholders—and not including them (or at least giving them a head's up) could lead to swift backlash. Unfortunately, given the power of social media today, backlash tends to become very public. I have had my fair share of backlash on college alumni Facebook groups, some that I couldn't avoid—and others that could have been mitigated had I included more alumni in my decision-making. Finally, don't forget that donors also can have an incredible amount of influence on campus politics. One swift move by an admission dean could mean a donor rescinds a gift or stops donating all together. I still remember proposing to eliminate an admission recruitment partnership on campus, only to learn from the development office that several alumni earmarked their donations specifically to that program. Anger ensued, and I spent weeks trying to find common ground with the donors. Sometimes the issues you are dealing with are so divisive, it is inevitable, but in my experience, most of these things can be avoided through courageous conversations, transparency, and relationship building with donors.

In fact, some of the most difficult conversations I've ever had in my career were with donors who disagreed with my direction. I always made a point to reach out to those donors directly and work on cultivating relationships. Despite our differences, there was always something we had in common—we cared deeply about the college and wanted the best for its future. If you start from a place of commonality, you will find that conversations are also places where the most people are willing to listen, and in some cases, even change their mind. It turns out that, in most cases where alumni or donors disagreed about my direction, not only were the conversations incredibly rewarding, but I actually ended up forming strong relationships with those individuals. Some of them even committed more funding for the college than they originally intended.

I will admit this part of the job isn't always easy. It often takes years of relationship building to navigate some of the politics of alumni and donors, but it is time well spent. The rewards can be transformative.

Inclusion and Transparency

Johnnie Johnson, vice president for enrollment management at Washington College, believes that in higher education, "Politicking is necessary, but it has to be genuine."

He arrived at Washington College in Maryland in September 2022. "I inherited 5 years of declining enrollment," he recalls. "Morale on campus was low and skepticism about our ability to get the job done was high."[5]

Having served as a vice president at Transylvania University in Kentucky prior to his arrival, Johnnie was experienced in the politics of small college campuses. He had also served on the NACAC board of directors during a time of major governance changes. He was one of the leading voices in overhauling the governance of the association and restoring its relationship with its twenty-three affiliate organizations. The process was contentious and challenging, yet Johnnie knew that, to succeed, he needed to build trust and lead with transparency.

So, when he got to Washington College, he immediately got to work. "There were some things that were low hanging fruit. I started with transparency. Believe it or not, it wasn't something the community was used to."[6] He quickly realized the faculty on campus did not receive regular updates from the admission office. So, he started attending faculty meetings and would share as much data and context as he could. "To be honest, a lot of the data wasn't uplifting, but I felt it was important to share it anyway," he explains. "If you are going to build a coalition to help with enrollment, that coalition first needs to have a clear picture of what the challenges are."[7] His approach is very much in line with John Kotter's very first rule of change management: create a sense of urgency.[8]

Although the data Johnnie shared were sobering, faculty became his biggest supporters. Many said to him, "No one ever shared this kind of information with us before. Now we understand the challenges that lie ahead. We want to help."

One piece of advice Johnnie offers any new admission dean is to use the language of "we."[9] From the minute you get on campus, make sure you own and take full responsibility for any challenges you inherit. Many leaders make the mistake of blaming their predecessors. "It's not a good look. My philosophy is, when I take a new job, the problems are now mine. The past is the past, my job is to move the community towards a future." Johnnie also made sure to use the term "we" the minute he arrived on campus, which I believe is incredibly wise, especially in a system of shared governance. Many leaders arrive on a campus and say things like, "You all have this challenge, or you all have done this in the past." The minute you step on campus, you are now part of the community. Use the word *we*, and don't make references to your previous institution. I've heard deans say, "At my previous institution, we used to do . . ."; this is a very quick way to isolate yourself from the community. When you arrive on campus, wear that new identity and shed your previous one. It shows that you are fully present and "all in."

Johnnie also realized he needed to create relationships with as many constituents on campus as possible. He took people out to dinner, ate in the dining hall, and worked to solidify relationships with trustees whom he knew had the biggest stakes in enrollment. His philosophy has always been "create relationships with the people that intimidate you."[10]

When you are a chief enrollment officer, especially in today's competitive landscape, you need everyone on the campus to feel a sense of urgency around enrollment. From the groundskeepers to the dining hall staff—everyone is a recruiter. Johnnie Johnson believes the key to success in enrollment leadership is to ensure everyone on campus understands the complexity and nuances of enrolling a class and feels inspired to work together. "You need every person on campus to champion your cause. When you are selling a $70,000 product, you need it to shine every day."[11]

Johnnie does this by creating relationships. And he doesn't just focus on faculty, administrative staff, and students—he knows there is real power in the staff who work behind the scenes. He eats in the dining hall and gets to know the food service staff, he gets to know the groundskeeping staff. He reminds them how important their jobs are and how they, too, are a part of the institution's success.

I had a similar experience when I worked at Trinity College. The wonderful woman who cleaned the admission building, Nancy Sanchez, would often say to me, "Angel, I'm so happy I'm assigned to this building on campus. I know that so much of the college's success is reliant on what happens in this building, so don't you worry, I will always make it shine!"[12] Nancy's energy was infectious, and she felt a great sense of pride in playing a key role in helping the institution succeed. As Johnnie Johnson notes, "The only way to succeed in enrollment management is by mobilizing the community. You want every single person on your campus to want to be a part of the success."[13]

Finally, Johnnie is aware that, despite all of the relationship building, there will still be members of the community who don't agree with your direction or get angry about a variety of things. "You can't take the criticism personally," he says. "Enrollment is high stakes, and everyone on campus has an opinion about it. When folks are upset, your job is to uncover why. The truth is, everyone wants to be heard—and as a leader, your number one job is to listen without judgement.

Your task is to comb through the noise and find out what sits below the surface. Sometimes, the anger is just hidden fear. Your job is to understand what the fear is and address it."[14]

In my experience, so much of navigating campus politics is about listening to the people at your institution. Once you understand the history of your campus, its culture, and power dynamics, politicking will become a reflex—especially if you've been intentional about building trust. However, there are also key strategies you can always rely on to become an astute politician.

Strategies for Navigating Politics in the Deanship

1. **From the minute you arrive, be all in.** "What we did at my previous institution" is never a good conversation starter. The new campus must be your campus. Wear the colors, learn the lingo, get up to speed on the institution's history and traditions, and make an effort to understand organizational dynamics so that you can quickly identify allies to bring forward your ideas.[15]
2. **Don't wait for a crisis to form relationships.** From the minute you arrive on campus, you must immediately begin to build relationships. Get to know who the key decision makers are on campus, invite them to a meal, stay in touch, and communicate regularly. To thrive in this job, you must genuinely enjoy building relationships. As Johnnie Johnson reminds us, "Politicking is necessary, but it should be genuine."[16] The key to leadership is the building of trust, and the way you build trust is through relationships. Make this your first priority when you arrive on a campus. Lee Coffin at Dartmouth states that he spent his first few years as dean "friend building." He wanted the community to know him and understand what he was working on; he listened to as much feedback as he could get.[17] If you wait until a crisis hits, or when you want to implement change, you will find yourself isolated. You will have a better chance at coming to consensus if the stakeholders who need to support you know and trust you and feel like you have a genuine interest in them and the institution. At the two campuses where I served as a dean, I immediately formed working relationships with the provost, the chair of the faculty senate, the head of the alumni board, the student government president, the editor of the student newspaper, the chair of the faculty admission committee, key trustees and

donors, the director of athletics, groundskeeping staff, and any other member of the community that had formal and informal influence. I genuinely enjoyed building these relationships and have formed some lifelong friendships as a result. Although navigating difficult situations on campus is never easy, having a relationship with these individuals made it achievable.

3. **Become a cheerleader.** Admission deans must be one of the biggest cheerleaders for the institution, and in order to cheer, you must be present. Make sure you attend athletic games, faculty lectures, alumni events, theater productions, art openings, and more. Wear the school colors with pride, eat lunch in the dining hall and the faculty lounge, and don't forget to promote the institution on social media. At Pitzer College, it was rare to see me on campus without something orange on (the school color). At Trinity, I wore blue and gold ties almost every day to represent school pride. Some deans see these gestures as optional. I never did. I quickly realized that if I didn't become a part of the community's co-curricular life, people would notice and begin to question my commitment to the institution. Most important, it's a lot of fun—so get out there and become the best cheerleader you can be!
4. **Build allies.** Before you introduce any major changes or propose new policies, it's important to build allies. Just like the US Speaker of the House rarely goes into a vote without knowing how most senators feel about an issue, you also should know how constituents feel about campus issues. Every key decision you make on campus should have supporters. For example, before I proposed moving Trinity College to a test-optional policy, I worked with the president, key trustees, faculty, alumni, and student leaders behind the scenes to make the case. Once they were on board, I knew they would become champions for the policy and would bring the rest of their colleagues along. Always work carefully behind the scenes with key constituents to build allyship around the issues you want to address on campus. And whatever you do—never make an announcement about your intentions to make a policy change without running it by key constituents. Nine times out of ten—even if the policy is a good one—it will fail. On a college campus, people will support what they help build and will challenge the issues they weren't consulted on.
5. **It can't be a zero-sum game.** Restaurateur Danny Meyer states, "Change works only when people believe it's happening for them, not to them."[18] As

a dean, before I proposed any changes, I would always ask myself, "How can this change be a win for others on campus?" For example, when I was working to expand our financial aid program on campus, the athletic coaches became some of my biggest supporters, because it meant recruiting top athletes who needed financial support to attend. When I wanted to implement a new technology system in our division, I would make sure the key stakeholders understood how it would simplify their workloads. No one ever wants to feel like change is "happening" to them. They want to understand it and feel like it's a win. So, the change you propose can't be a zero-sum game. Help others see how they, too, will win.

6. **Get used to saying no.** Kasey Urquidez of the University of Arizona admits that the role of admission deans is tough for people pleasers. "You can't please everybody and that will make you uncomfortable—but it's the nature of the job."[19] Adele C. Brumfield at the University of Michigan knows this well. "Get used to not giving everyone everything they want. In order to succeed you're going to have to be comfortable saying no, a lot."[20]
7. **Focus on the moveable middle.** When you need to make change, don't waste your time and energy on the constituents who will never be convinced. Every campus I've worked on had stakeholders who would vote against anything I proposed—regardless of how good it was for the institution and students. In fact, former President of Macalester College Brian Rosenberg showcases this phenomenon in his book, *"Whatever It Is, I'm Against It."*[21] So, when I wanted to effect change on campus, I would focus on mobilizing what I call the moveable middle—these are the people open to being persuaded. I would meet with them individually and in groups and provide the data, background, and information they needed to understand the context. Storytelling is critical in these roles (hence the focus of the previous chapter in this book). Often, the moveable middle would become my greatest allies, and as a result, my proposals would pass through the college's governance systems.
8. **Poke holes in everything.** Before you put something in front of any constituency, make sure you study it from every angle, and try to get other people on your team to help you see things you may not see. Be your own devil's advocate—or invite a colleague to do it for you. Ashley Perzyna, who served as chief of staff for several college presidents (and is now

NACAC's chief operating officer, makes this an essential part of her professional practice. Regardless of what project she's working on, she adopts a healthy skepticism to make sure she examines it critically before presenting it. She says, "The notion of poking holes in everything refers to my desire to view an issue from every perspective—challenging and attempting to discredit an argument or recommendation in the spirit of making it stronger. It has always been my job to find the blind spots in any project or proposal."[22] One of the ways I do this is by showing my leadership team and other people in the organization PowerPoint presentations or reports I am going to share with the board or other leadership groups, in advance of the meetings. The leadership team helps me strengthen my arguments and often catches things I would not have seen.

9. **Listen with intent.** In his book *Humble Inquiry*, Edgar H. Schein defines "humble inquiry" as "the fine art of drawing someone out, of asking questions to which you do not already know the answer, or building a relationship based on curiosity and interest in the other person."[23] So often, as leaders, we spend a lot of time working to persuade others of our perspective. But one of the most important things we need to learn is how to listen to others—and I mean truly listen. We are also quick to be defensive when criticism comes our way. Satyajit Dattagupta at Northeastern University always reminds himself to remove his ego when criticism comes his way. He states, "I have to detach myself from my emotions and ask myself, what are people really saying here? It's more important to listen than to hold on to your desire not to be wrong."[24] How many times have we found ourselves in a conversation with someone at work, and while they are speaking, we are already processing how we are going to respond to them? Well, at that moment, we are not truly listening. One of the best ways to build trust and break through some of the challenges you will face in a shared governance system is to truly listen to constituents with true curiosity and no preconceived notions. It's a challenging skill to learn, but when you do, it will transform your relationships, and it will help you get information you never would have had access to. I highly recommend reading Schein's book. It will help you hone the skill of humble inquiry.
10. **Compromise is key.** A strategy I often use when trying to navigate politics is to go into every situation assuming I won't get everything

I want. Often, leaders go into negotiations ready for battle, and they feel unsuccessful if they don't get everything they want. If you go into each negotiation, strategy meeting, or leadership presentation assuming there will be some aspects of your plan that will work and others that you will simply have to give up, you will always leave with a feeling of accomplishment. Institutions of higher education are highly political environments, which means compromise is the way to move your agenda forward.

Poking Holes

I wish I had, years ago, adhered to Ashley Perzyna's advice about poking holes. I learned my lesson the hard way. At NACAC's national conference in 2021, I delivered a state of the association speech. I reviewed the PowerPoint presentation many times before delivering the speech. In my mind, the slides were flawless. However, as I delivered my speech, I showed a slide that highlighted the demographics of our membership. I somehow forgot to include data about Asian Americans and Pacific Islanders (AAPI). There were thousands of people in the audience, and some immediately noticed. Members took to social media immediately to condemn my presentation. The NACAC AAPI special interest group has a Facebook page with several hundred members. Members began sharing their outrage on the page and called for the creation of a petition against me. My email and social media inboxes immediately began to flood with messages from the audience, who claimed I did not care about our AAPI members. Pretty soon the message got out that I did not include AAPI members in my presentation, and people who were not even present at the conference joined the chorus of anger on social media. The situation took many hours of my time during the conference and sensitive handling during the weeks following. I was devastated then and still feel devastated today. I can't believe I didn't have other people look at my presentation and poke holes in it. My intention is to never exclude anyone, and I clearly missed the mark. This situation could've been easily avoided had I adopted a healthy skepticism about my own presentation and asked others for feedback.

Curiosity, not Anger

Even while using these ten strategies for navigating politics, it is inevitable you will need to have difficult conversations and hear troubling feedback and perspectives from your supervisors, colleagues, and other constituents and stakeholders. In his book *How to Know a Person: The Art of Seeing Others Deeply and Being Deeply Seen*, *The New York Times* columnist David Brooks gives important advice for how to handle difficult conversations. He notes that when people approach us with anger or frustration, most of us get defensive. He writes: "It's best to avoid this temptation. As soon as somebody starts talking about times when they felt excluded, betrayed, or wronged, stop and listen. When somebody is talking to you about pain in their life, even in those cases when you may think their pain is performative or exaggerated, it's best not to try to yank the conversations back to your frame."[25]

Instead, it's much more productive to step into the other person's shoes and get comfortable there for a while to try to see how the situation looks to them from their perspective. Listen deeply to what they have to say and encourage them to say more. The more you can make yourself curious about what they have to say, the better you'll be able to maintain a productive line of communication, even in the most stressful of circumstances.

In all my leadership roles, I have always tried to take this approach. I will admit it's never been easy, but I'm determined to master this skill. I still remember my second week on the job at NACAC and attending my first meeting with the presidents of our twenty-three affiliate organizations. I was not prepared for the anger they greeted me with. They were upset with a lack of transparency in the organization and clearly were frustrated with the way the organization made decisions in the past. There was so much I didn't understand, given it was only my second week on the job. However, the issues were now mine to deal with, and I wasn't concerned about the past. My job was to move us forward. But for about two hours, I listened and asked as many questions as they asked me.

At one point during the conversation, I said to the group, "I understand you are all frustrated, but my leadership style is about assuming best intentions." The minute I said that, it was clear I had hit a nerve. For the next hour the group shared their anger about how the organization did not show them best intentions. Instead of being defensive, I took a gentle approach and asked inquisitive questions.

I approached the session through a spirit of inquiry. The minute I left the meeting, I made a commitment to personally calling as many current and former affiliate presidents as possible to discuss the matter. I asked them to go deeper in their storytelling, to help me understand where the anger was coming from. I did not show emotion during those conversations, and I certainly did not take their anger personally. I listened, took notes, thanked them for their input, and promised I would work to build trust in the organization. I made it a point to step into their shoes and try to understand the situation from their perspective. As I spoke to more people, I realized many of them had been hurt by the association and NACAC did indeed have a long way to go before it could rebuild trust. It took us a few years, but we now enjoy a strong working relationship with our affiliate presidents.

It's difficult to make significant progress as a leader if you don't control your ego. Instead of allowing your emotions to dictate how you respond to situations, allow your curiosity to do so instead. I admit this is often difficult to do. You will find that in leadership roles, many people will not approach you with kindness. As Adele C. Brumfield at University of Michigan told me, "My goal is always to give people grace, even when it isn't being extended to me."[26] I follow a similar philosophy. I have a quote written in my daily journal that reads, "When you have the choice to be right or to be kind, always pick kind."

Mark Steinlage, vice president for enrollment management at Rockhurst University, takes a very similar approach to difficult conversations. In fact, his response strategy is based on his own upbringing in Jesuit education. As he guides his staff and community through challenging conversations, he uses the Ignatian Principles of Conversation to lead those discussions. I have witnessed him using these as he also navigated contentious politics in his role as a NACAC board director and have seen the powerful impact these principles can have. Mark often shares these principles with audiences before engaging in difficult or challenging discussions and asks that everyone adhere to them. I found them to be very powerful and would like to share them with you as well:

- Be slow to speak.
- Listen attentively.
- Seek the truth in what others are saying.
- Disagree humbly, respectfully, and thoughtfully.
- Allow the conversation the time it needs.[27]

Advice from the Deans

On Becoming an Astute Politician

Every dean I interviewed recognizes that being an astute politician is not something they were taught, but the skill grew with experience. They all agree leading through inclusivity, listening more than speaking, and checking your ego at the door are keys to their success.

> One of the worst things you can do as a new dean is burn human capital. So many walk into an institution and want to implement hardwire change. You can't force change, because if you do you will burn through a lot of your political capital. Take the long view, and don't rush.
>
> —Satyajit Dattagupta, executive vice chancellor, chief enrollment officer, and senior advisor to the president, Northeastern University[28]

> Don't have difficult conversations on email. Walk over to people's offices and talk. Things will get resolved more quickly, and you will avoid a lot of misinterpretation.
>
> —Kasey Urquidez, former vice president, enrollment management, and dean, admissions, University of Arizona[29]

> Being present on campus isn't just for show. It helps you form a core for your storytelling. Whether your stories are for prospective students and their supporters, or for your campus colleagues, they are more credible when they are infused with deep details from the institution you represent.
>
> —Ken Anselment, former vice president for enrollment and communication at Lawrence University[30]

> I am very careful about what I say as a dean. I know that what I say has a significant amount of weight on campus. I have to navigate politics carefully, so I ask myself, "How will this message be received? How might it be interpreted, what is my intention?" When I pause and ask myself these questions, my approach may be different.
>
> —Fumio Sugihara, dean of admissions and financial aid, Hampshire College[31]

I try to listen more than I speak. This way I find that when I speak, it's informed and most people are ready to listen.

—J. T. Duck, dean of admissions, Tufts University[32]

Check your ego at the door in this job. I've seen many people who come into the deanship with ego, and they crash and burn. These jobs require humility. If you are going to build trust and move people towards your cause, you must be humble.

—Mark Steinlage, vice president of enrollment management, Rockhurst University[33]

There are people on campus who are tightly connected to the underground information chain, and it's important to tap into those people to understand what's going on below the surface. At the same time, you have to be careful about what—and about how much—you contribute to that network, and caution is essential. It's also important to know that the most vocal people are likely to be the first to bring you their problems, opinions, and "helpful" suggestions about how to do your job; while it's important to listen, of course, being first in line doesn't make them right. Getting alternative opinions is critical for leaders to understand the whole picture.

—Jon Boeckenstedt, vice provost of enrollment management, Oregon State University[34]

Astute politicians step into the margins. What I mean by that is that they are willing to go beyond the obvious in a situation and ask themselves, "Where did this come from? What is the real reason for the concern behind these issues? How can I build more trust and credibility by addressing the cause and not the symptom?

—Mark Steinlage, vice president of enrollment management, Rockhurst University[35]

CHAPTER 5

Leading in Crisis

A search consultant I spoke to recently said, "Anyone who served as a leader during the pandemic led in dog years." It may only have been two years of leadership, but to the body and soul, it felt like eight. I became CEO of NACAC in July 2020. We were in the midst of a global pandemic, which presented many organizations with some of the greatest challenges they've ever faced. The US was also in a tense period of racial reckoning after the brutal murders of George Floyd and Breonna Taylor within months of each other.[1] Like students on college campuses who channeled their anger at their administrators—demanding systemic change against injustice—many NACAC members turned to the board and me, expecting systemic change in the organization and in the college admission counseling profession. This response didn't surprise me. When people are angry at the world, most turn to the organizations in which they feel they have a voice—it's where they feel they can make an impact.

Anyone who takes on a leadership role should expect they will eventually be faced with the same kind of pressure. In fact, Kathleen McCartney, former president of Smith College, writes about this in an *Inside Higher Ed* column: "A clinical psychologist once commented that a college president is a public transference figure, meaning people will transfer unresolved, unconscious conflicts in their lives to you."[2] I certainly experienced this in 2020 and throughout my entire time in leadership.

Like so many organizations, NACAC was also facing a significant financial crisis during the pandemic. The majority of our revenue was generated from in-person programming, and our losses were steep. Within a few weeks of my arrival, it was clear that to protect the organization's future, I would need to lay off a third of the staff and significantly cut operating expenses.

In addition, the US Department of Justice had recently filed a lawsuit against NACAC, claiming that sections of our ethical code violated anti-trust laws. The organization was forced to settle with the department, removing ethical guidelines that members felt were good for students.[3] Morale across the membership was at an all-time low. I knew we had to make changes quickly, but the organization's outdated, complex governance structure prevented us from doing so. We had an assembly of 215 delegates, several standing committees, 69 presidents of our state and regional affiliate organizations, a 16-member board of directors, and many other informal groups who felt like they had the right to govern the organization. Although this structure had served NACAC well in the past, unprecedented challenges made it clear that it needed a major overhaul. If the association were to thrive in a complex new world, it needed a nimbler governance system.

Organizational change, especially governance changes, are often met with skepticism and anger, and ours was no different. As the NACAC board and I tackled governance changes and addressed many crises simultaneously, the vitriol arrived in very public settings—social media, online conferences, town halls, and more. The world felt heavy, and it didn't help that the college admission counseling profession was experiencing some of the most unprecedented shifts in its history.[4]

I'm happy to report that careful and strategic stewardship helped NACAC weather the storm and emerge stronger. But if it weren't for strategically focusing on principles of leading in crisis and managing organizational change (some of which I discuss in this chapter), NACAC would be in a very different position today.

Although the situation I walked into at NACAC felt like "the perfect storm," it's not uncommon. Every leader will inevitably experience their own storms, and admission deans are no exception. Leading in times of crisis will be an inevitable part of the deanship, which is why it's important to address this timely topic. In this chapter, I outline key strategies to approach crisis strategically while inspiring others and managing your own reactions and responses to difficult situations.

Leading in crisis requires a balance of tactics, strategy, mindset, and self-management. In a crisis, I find many leaders put all their energies toward building a strategy and operationalizing it. However, your mindset (your attitude or set of beliefs) and self-management (how you compose yourself and take responsibility for your own behavior and well-being) are two of the most important strategies required to succeed in today's complicated landscape.

At the time I'm writing this book, colleges are dealing with the fallout of the botched Free Application for Federal Student Aid (FAFSA) rollout in 2024, making it difficult to predict how many students will enroll next year, and putting institutional revenue at risk. For some institutions already suffering from enrollment challenges, the FAFSA rollout has had devastating consequences.[5] This is added on top of the declining perception of higher education in America; a demographic cliff (including a million students lost in the pipeline during the COVID-19 pandemic); legislation opposing diversity, equity, and inclusion in many states; disagreement regarding admission testing policies; and divisive campus protests about the Israel-Hamas war, all of which have created a new perfect storm for admission leaders.[6] In fact, some colleges have already reported they enrolled fewer students as a result of student protests on campus and interrupted tours where students were actively telling prospective families not to enroll at the institution.[7]

Admission deans won't always know what crisis will land at their doorsteps, but it's important to have several guiding principles they can turn to. These principles can guide your approach, decision-making, and strategy. The following are a few that have guided me and other admission leaders during our most difficult moments. I urge any dean to spend time thinking through crisis management scenarios before they actually are faced with a challenge. Although leading in crisis is always challenging, it's easier to navigate when you have principles you can rely on when crisis hits. Committing to those principles now is an important step in preparation.

PRINCIPLES FOR CRISIS LEADERSHIP IN ADMISSIONS

Be Optimistic

Regardless of how challenging the crisis is, admission deans must lead with optimism. To be clear, that does not mean promising things you can't deliver or being naïve about the reality of the challenges. Optimism is about instilling hope for the future and being transparent about what the organization faces. Leaders set the tone, and your most important responsibility is to convey a sense of hope and direction. If you are negative, your team will be, too.

Disney CEO Bob Iger, the ultimate optimist, was one of my greatest inspirations in moments when I led in crisis. In his book *The Ride of a Lifetime*, he reminds us that: "If you walk up and down the halls constantly telling people, 'The sky is falling,' a sense of doom and gloom will, over time, permeate the company. You can't communicate pessimism to the people around you. It's ruinous to morale. No one wants to follow a pessimist."[8]

This is why, despite all the challenges NACAC faced when I arrived, I always tried to give the team, the board, and the membership a sense of hope. Every opportunity I got, I tried to paint a picture of what progress could look like if we all worked together. Although I certainly didn't have all the answers and couldn't guarantee what the future held, I made sure to constantly remind my constituents we were working toward progress and change and within every crisis lies opportunity.

Optimism is a skill set that can challenge leaders. It is easy to be overwhelmed in a crisis and feel like the weight of the world is on your shoulders. However, you can't allow those feelings to paralyze you, and you certainly can't share them with your teams. I want to be clear: I'm not saying you shouldn't be a human being. All of us feel down when we are deeply challenged, but as the leader of your organization, you must project optimism, even when it does not feel natural. During the hardest moments in your organization, everyone is relying on you for a sense of hope.

Fumio Sugihara was the dean of admissions and financial aid at Marlboro College, which closed in 2020. He knew the institution was having significant enrollment and financial challenges when he arrived. However, he was passionate about the mission of the institution and felt he could make a difference there. Despite the extraordinary challenges, he always led with optimism. He knew his most important job was to motivate a team of admission counselors to enroll a class. He also knew all eyes were on them, and sometimes the work felt defeating. He said, "You have to give people a north star. I constantly reminded my team that we had the honor of doing something most admission officers don't get to do—save a college."[9] That kind of reframing energized his team, and although the college eventually did close, his counselors were committed and hopeful right until the end.

Sometimes being optimistic takes a toll on leaders. As a dean, there were days I felt exhausted by having to "put on a brave face," even when it didn't feel genuine. Because all of us need outlets where we can express our fears and frustrations, it's important to build a network with whom you can confidentially share these emotions. I relied on peers at other institutions whom I had forged strong relationships with. I relied on some of my mentors who had trained me in the field. When Ken Anselment was the vice president for enrollment and communication at Lawrence University, he convened a monthly conversation with his fellow enrollment leaders in the Associated Colleges of the Midwest. An avid cyclist, he called the group "the ACM Enrollment Leaders Group Ride," emphasizing the power of a group of fellow travelers riding together—often into headwinds or up steep hills. They would discuss shared challenges and celebrations, reinforcing that riding with others is easier than riding alone. Today, I work with an executive coach, who often helps me navigate difficult moments, and I turn to peers who lead other organizations. When you become a dean, find trusted friends and colleagues who can support you through the difficult moments so that you can show up for your teams resilient, hopeful, and optimistic.

Overcommunicate

Most leaders don't communicate enough when times are good. During a crisis, you must overcommunicate. People need to know where you are going, why you are making these decisions, and what your intentions are. During my time as a leader, I have found that communication is one of the most important tools you have to help organizations manage a crisis. Your ability to help your constituents understand what is happening and how you might be addressing it will help mitigate rumors or make situations worse. As author Britt Andreatta astutely observes, "Psychologists have long known that in the absence of information, the brain fills in the blanks. But it doesn't just fill in any story. According to psychologist Dr. Janice Rudestam, the brain fills in the worst-case scenario."[10] During a crisis, it's important to communicate immediately, even if you don't have all the answers—and the truth is, you never will. In every crisis I've ever handled, I have followed three guiding principles for communicating. They are the three things my constituency needs to understand: (1) What do I know right now? (2) What am I working on? and (3) What are the next steps?

It's important to admit you don't have all the answers and you will reach back out when you know more. Often, leaders wait too long to communicate because they feel all the pieces of the puzzle must have come together before doing so. In our fast-paced world where everyone can comment immediately on social media, it's important for leaders to communicate—even if it's just to say, "We are aware of the situation, we are working on it, and when we know more, we will be in touch." If you don't tell the story, others will do it for you, and they'll usually have it wrong.

Empower Your Team

Every crisis is an opportunity to help your team grow into their own leadership. In the book *The Prepared Leader*, the authors note, "In jazz ensembles, every player takes a turn to lead with their instrument. . . . Leadership rotates as the music dictates, and players often improvise, taking cues from each other's performance. For the whole thing to work, each player must listen to what the other musicians are playing at the same time. They must truly hear and understand what the music is saying to them—what it is telling them—to be able to decide what notes or harmonies to play next."[11]

Often, deans of admission feel they need to have all the answers, but the truth is, no one individual ever does. You will have blind spots and biases like everyone else, and the most important decisions require diverse perspectives. In fact, research shows that diverse teams make better decisions up to 87 percent of the time.[12]

You also have to remember that, as a leader, you are not alone. You need the good counsel of others. If you make decisions in a silo, you won't succeed. Before you make a difficult decision, seek the confidential advice of your team. This is one of the reasons why building the right team is so essential. It's important to understand the individual strengths of each of your team members. It will help you decipher whom to lean on when. For example, you may be facing a crisis that requires careful storytelling, or someone who can attend to small details with great care. You need to know whom the people on your team are that you can call on when these are the skills that will help mitigate your crisis. In addition, it's important to know who on your team responds most calmly in a crisis. Pull those individuals close to you in times of crisis. They will help you see the forest from the trees without adding emotionality to the situation.

In *The Prepared Leader*, the authors also note: "In the midst of a crisis is when you will really understand whether or not you have the right diversity of skill set on your teams. You want to make sure you have people who think about and approach problem solving differently. You don't want to wait until crisis arises to develop a strong, diverse team."[13]

In my experience, teams who have built trust tend to work better under pressure—and respond to crisis with greater ease. The building of trust does not happen overnight. Creating a high-performing team takes years and requires a serious commitment on the leader's part. In every leadership role I have held, I have invested in my teams. We go on retreats together, we share personality assessments (which help us understand each other's character traits), we create time and space to talk about our own strengths and weaknesses, and we create a set of principles and values that we all agree to abide by. Crises are difficult enough to deal with, so you want to avoid bringing unhealthy dynamics into the situation. The way you build trust is by intentionally investing in your teams. This will ensure that when the going gets tough, each team member will bring their best to the situation.

Finally, it's important to note, as a leader, you will be the person ultimately responsible for final decision-making, especially during a crisis. I firmly believe you must trust your gut. Take all the advice you can from your team, and when appropriate, follow that advice. Yet, other times, your gut will tell you that you need to do something different. Throughout my career, the only times I have felt regret about a decision is when I took the advice of my team, despite the fact my gut was telling me I should move in a different direction. I believe we need to follow our intuition, and the only way to do that is to sit in silence (you will learn more about this in chapter 6). When you need to make an important decision, seek all the counsel you can get, study the issue from different perspectives, but in the end, listen to your inner voice. That voice is pointing you in the right direction. When I haven't listened to that voice is when I've made poor decisions.

For example, I once hired a person on my team who turned out to be a disaster. I actually knew from the minute I interviewed this person they were not a good fit with my leadership style, but I felt a lot of pressure from other members of my team to hire this person. The situation did not work out, and as a result, it was one of my most stressful years. Despite all of the advice you receive, remember you are the one ultimately responsible for the decision. As one of my board members, Tahirah Crawford, reminds me when I am faced with difficult decisions,

"You are the one who needs to be able to sleep at night. Make the decision that will bring you the most peace."[14]

How Do I Want This Moment to Be Remembered?

One of my guiding principles in a crisis is to ask myself: How do I want this moment to be remembered? In the heat of a crisis, you can reframe your decision-making by pausing and asking yourself, "If I were to reflect on this moment five years from now, what would I want to be proud of?" In 2020, I asked myself this before I laid off a third of my team at NACAC. Even though it was one of the darkest days of my career, I wanted to make sure everyone who was impacted by my decision felt I did it with kindness, grace, and respect. Although the news I was delivering wasn't going to be easy to receive, I wanted them to feel dignity. Although you never know how your actions will impact people, your intentions matter and delivery matters.

Satyajit at Northeastern has a similar strategy. When he served as the dean of admission at Tulane University, the university sent admit letters to 130 students that had not been admitted to the college. The higher education media immediately caught wind of it, turning it into a crisis. The team was feeling deflated, and Satyajit was determined to support them. He told them the next few days would probably be some of the most difficult they had experienced. He knew the kind of scrutiny and outrage this mistake would bring. He reminded them, however, it would pass and eventually would be okay. He encouraged everyone to come together to support each other. In an interview for this book, he said, "Having clarity of vision during a crisis is so important. You need to remind people that while things are hard now, they won't always be. You also need to ask yourself, is this something I will care about in five years? When you take that perspective, you realize the emotions are only temporary."[15]

Adele C. Brumfield was in leadership at the University of California San Diego (UCSD) during the pandemic. Like most institutions, UCSD had to furlough employees to ensure financial sustainability for the organization. One of the strategies Adele used was to advocate for her admissions team to be classified as essential employees. This meant employees would have to come into the office on a regular basis. It sparked immediate backlash. What the staff didn't realize at the time, and what Adele couldn't tell them, is that she was using this as a strategy to ensure that her team was not impacted by layoffs. She felt her team may have a smaller likelihood of being laid off if they were essential employees. In the end, her entire team were able to keep their jobs during the pandemic. Most now reflect on the moment with gratitude, yet it certainly didn't feel that way at the time. One of the things most leaders struggle with is that their intentions can't always be made public. Adele was willing to take the heat in the moment when she made the decision, but in the back of her mind, she was focused on the larger goal, which was to put UCSD in a position to thrive in a pandemic and to simultaneously care for her team. She also took the long view and considered how she wanted the decision to be remembered.

"Your job as a leader is to be focused on the end game, not the challenge of the day," Adele reflects. "Your job is to cut through the noise and help people find perspective. It's not always easy, but you must project calm at all times. It's also important to show a little vulnerability, to ensure that you share your humanity. You don't want your team to think that you aren't impacted by the crisis, but all eyes are on you, and you must always be the calmest person in the room."[16]

Equanimity

Because I have seen so many leaders on college campuses lose their temper, I think it's important to repeat Adele's wisdom: Regardless of how challenging the situation is, you must always be the calmest person in the room. As Dale Elwood, former dean of the Harvard Kennedy school would say, "Keep smiling, regardless of the context, because leaders set the tone for their institutions. And I have, in fact, come to believe that setting the tone is one of the leader's most important tasks."[17] Leaders must find calm in the midst of the storm, and there is no way of leaders losing respect faster than losing their cool.

Being the calmest person in the room is a skill that can be learned. The following are a few strategies I've used that I hope are helpful to you.

Take a Bird's Eye View. I have a practice I use every time I am facing a difficult situation where I feel pressured or "under fire." I float above the room. Although I am still physically present in the room, I pretend I am slowly floating above it and looking down at the situation from above. It allows me to feel a sense of distance from the tension and not take things personally. It allows me to be calm, and often, it even allows me to find humor in the situation.

When I was a dean at Trinity College, I used this strategy often. I still remember walking into a meeting with all the athletic coaches who were frustrated with new admission policies and processes I was implementing and felt a sense of fear they would impact their teams negatively. I knew it was going to be a tense meeting, so before I walked into the athletics center, I snuck into a bathroom in the building next door, closed my eyes, and did some deep breathing. I often do breathing exercises or meditation before I walk into meetings I know may be tense.

As I sat in the front of the room with dozens of coaches in front of me, I listened for about an hour as, one by one, they rose and shared their frustrations. Some were kind, others were angry, most were unhappy. While I sat there "taking the heat," I floated above the room. I watched myself observing the situation, and although I was present and listening, it was a way of distancing myself from the situation. It allowed me to remain calm, and none of the things that were said angered me personally. As I observed the situation from "up above," the distance allowed me to focus on the fact that this situation was not about me. It was about the role I played at the institution. I slowly floated back down from the room as the meeting was ending. On the way out, one of my staff members (the admission athletics liaison who was in the room) put his arm over my shoulder and said, "Are you ok? Wow, that was brutal." I replied, "I feel absolutely fine, shall we go grab a drink at happy hour?"

One of the things many of my colleagues told me when I left Trinity to become NACAC CEO is they admired how calm I had remained under incredibly difficult circumstances. Many had observed me in meetings throughout my tenure at the college where constituents were unhappy, but they noted I always listened, never lost my calm, and was always respectful. That was always my intention. And it's also how I wanted those moments to be remembered.

Practice Detachment. The example I just described is also known as professional detachment—the notion of an appropriate emotional distance from a particular situation at work.[18] I have evolved in my own leadership and now commit to not taking anything personally at work. Although I am often faced with challenging situations, and people have certainly said mean things to me, I try to maintain a healthy distance by reminding myself that I am not the role. So often, leaders get upset when their constituents express anger, frustration, or discontent. It's important to understand this is to be expected when you move into these roles. However, reminding yourself you represent a role, you are not THE role, is critical. It will help you maintain a sense of calm and allow a healthy distance between you and the situation at hand. Joseph Montgomery at North

Carolina A&T has honed this skill by sitting in silence during tense moments or when topics are being discussed that he disagrees with. "I have to admit, I didn't always get that right, but over time I've learned to manage my emotional response," he shares. "You don't want everyone in the room to know how you feel about a situation, and you can't be in defensive mode."[19] Whitney Soule at the University of Pennsylvania, who has had to manage many difficult situations since her arrival, practices detachment often. She notes, "When anger comes my way, I try to remember that anyone sitting in this chair would receive this anger. I realize that the outrage is directed at the role, not the individual."[20]

Slow Down. Slowing down in a crisis feels counterintuitive. Deans will feel pressure to have the answers immediately. However, you rarely have to respond in the moment, and you should always give yourself the time to think and process.

For example, Whitney Soule at the University of Pennsylvania feels strongly about taking time to make decisions. Reflecting on her first deanship at Bowdoin College, she says,

> I realized pretty quickly that the final decision always rested with me. That can feel like a pretty heavy burden, so I always want to be thoughtful and intentional about how I confront difficult situations. I insist on slowing down and taking a pause before making decisions. It allows me to consider all the possible implications. I also recognize that the decisions I make are not just about the situation, but it's also about my leadership style. Everyone is always watching to see how I lead, and I want to make sure the decisions I make represent my values, and the institution's values.[21]

In a similar fashion, I also make a practice of slowing down when everyone around me speeds up. In fact, my usual response when a member of my team approaches me with a perceived crisis is, "Let me sit with this." I try to give myself distance before tackling the issue. I often try to give myself an evening or an entire day (more if possible) before I have to make important decisions. That distance allows me time to think, consult others, and examine implications. It also allows me to think about how I may want to communicate my decision and what it might say about my leadership or values. I continuously ask myself, "What does this decision say about my values? About my leadership?" The answers often come to me during a morning meditation or a long run. You won't always have a day or a few hours to make a decision, but you should always take a few minutes to pause, breathe, and go quiet before you react. Don't allow others to pressure you into making important decisions on their timeline. In fact, create a culture in your office where the most important decisions always require a pause.

Another important way to practice pausing is to take time to think before you respond to emails. Most of us have sent emails we regret because we allowed our emotions to get in the way. In his masterclass, in which he teaches about stoic philosophy, Ryan Holiday teaches that "delay is the best remedy for anger."[22] I have learned to take an intentional pause before I respond emotionally to any circumstance; it always results in a more thoughtful, less emotional outcome. This includes email. In my experience, any email I draft and come back to a day later never looks the same by the time I send it. It's always softer and gentler and contains less emotion. J. T. Duck at Tufts University says, "I've gotten really good about not sending the email that I've written and giving myself time to process it. A younger me would've written that email and sent it right away. I now realize that pausing and giving myself time to figure out what my end game is more important than responding with emotion."[23]

Lead with Your Mission and Values. When faced with difficult situations, you must always lean on your mission and values. These are your North Star and should guide your decision-making. When I joined NACAC and realized we were going to have to make some heart-wrenching financial sacrifices, I asked my team to come together for a budget retreat. Of course, we wore masks and sat six feet apart, but we felt that such critical decision-making required us to be together.

Before the team arrived, I put our mission statement on the wall. Then I took huge sticky notes and posted our values all over the walls. When the team arrived, I told them what our charge was. We needed to find cost savings to ensure the financial sustainability of the organization. The caveat, however, was nothing we cut could put our mission or values at risk.

It was a challenging day, but in the end, it was also one of the most inspiring. Every time we discussed an expense to potentially eliminate, we would ask ourselves, how does this impact our mission and does eliminating it threaten our values? Despite what seemed like a herculean task, we found the expenses we needed to cut, and we also made decisions about where to invest strategically. I believe you can't cut your way to greatness, so in the spirit of upholding our mission, we cut areas to invest in others. The team came together to solve an organizational challenge, but we did so by ensuring the mission of the organization went unharmed.

Never Let a Crisis Go to Waste. In *The Prepared Leader*, the authors note: "For most of us, crises are predominantly threats. We are inclined to frame them as danger—to ourselves, our people, our organizations, and our stakeholders. But crises are ambiguous. They are both threats and opportunities."[24]

This is why one of my core guiding principles during a crisis is to always look for the opportunity. When I've had to cut budgets, for example, I ask myself, "What are the opportunities to learn to do the work differently, or to become more efficient? What can we cut that no longer serves us to invest in new opportunities?" When I've had to deliver difficult news to staff or board members, I asked myself, "How can I use this as an opportunity to showcase our values in action and create a vision for a different future?

The Prepared Leader posits nine skills of crisis management, which I find are particularly important for admission deans today:

1. **Sense-making:** Collect the facts and gather as many people as possible to understand the situation.
2. **Perspective taking:** Try to look at the situation from as many angles as possible, and bring in many different perspectives so that you are not biased.
3. **Influence:** The only power you have in a crisis is the power of influence. Your job is to inspire others toward action.
4. **Organizational agility:** How nimble is your organization, and what kind of bureaucracy exists in the decision-making process? The more agile you are, the faster you will be able to respond to crisis. A perfect example of a lack of agility was NACAC's former governance structure.
5. **Creativity:** Have you cultivated a culture of creativity and "out of the box" thinking to solve challenges?
6. **Communicating effectively:** You must share information with your constituents as quickly as you can, create a sense of urgency, and also inspire hope.
7. **Risk-taking:** Developing a tolerance for risk is key to success. All situations come with some form of risk.
8. **Promoting resilience:** Investing in your teams is the best way to ensure organizational resilience. Your staff is your greatest asset.

9. **Individual and systemic learning:** After the crisis, step back from the situation, process with your teams, take lessons learned, and discuss future scenarios.[25]

Recognize and Manage Underlying Emotions. One of the things I have come to learn as a leader across various organizations is you will be the recipient of the emotions of many constituents. I have been on the front lines of anger, even vitriol. In the book *Leader as Healer*, Nicholas Janni notes, "Very often, anger conceals grief or fear."[26] This is why I never take the emotions people share with me personally, and I certainly don't respond with anger. What has helped me over time is realizing below the anger or emotion is something deeper—it's fear or loss. When you are confronted with emotion from your constituents, ask yourself, What are the underlying issues creating these emotions?

When the remaining NACAC staff was angry at me because I laid off a third of our team, they were grieving the loss of their colleagues and fearing for their own jobs. When the faculty at Trinity College spent two hours at a town hall berating me and the president about our plans to "right size" the student body—the anger was really fear. Fear of a loss of revenue, which could mean cuts to their departmental budgets or salaries (none of their assumptions were true, but the fear was there nonetheless).

When members of my current leadership team come to me with anxiety during our budgeting season—to propose budget increases for their departments or raises for their staff members—the anxiety they exhibit is clearly fear. These fears may be they will have to have difficult conversations with their own employees or they will not have enough resources to deliver on the organization's goals. It could be fear that the results may be something they cannot support or a loss of power in decision-making.

As a leader, your job is to figure out what lies below the anger and anxiety people approach you with on a regular basis. In every situation where emotions are high, I always ask myself, "Why is this person really behaving this way? What is below this emotion?" It allows me to distance myself from the situation and not respond with emotion. It also allows me to have a deeper level of empathy for the other individual(s) involved. I find when I try to uncover what is underlying the emotion, I am able to respond with a greater sense of clarity.

Spot Real Versus Perceived Crises. You will need to decide which situations require your attention and which do not. When you are in a leadership role, every day, people will bring you what I call "perceived crises." You will also find some of your own staff members or cabinet-level peers regularly bring you crises and find this way of operating "normal." Your job as a leader is to decide what rises to the level of "having to be dealt with" and what does not.

One way to accomplish this is to remember that not everything that lands at your desk has to be responded to, and not everything you are presented with has to be addressed immediately. If you ask anyone who has worked with me in the past, they'll tell you one of the things I constantly ask when they bring me perceived crises is, "Is this the hill you want to die on?" In other words, is this where you want to expend your energy or political capital?

I also ask, "Is this something that we need to deal with right now?" When you first join an organization, many of your constituents (especially your staff members) will want you to address every challenge immediately. I certainly felt that pressure when I arrived at NACAC. Everything felt urgent, and every meeting I had presented me with another "problem" to fix. My job was to cut through the noise and figure out what really needed to be addressed immediately and what could be dealt with over time. I still remember sitting with my chief of staff at the time, who brought me an endless number of perceived crises on a daily basis. One day I looked at her, with all sincerity, and said, "If I tackle all of these issues at the same time, I'll be dead in a year."

Of course, I was kidding, but she got the point. I've learned if you take everything on at the same time, you will run out of energy, exhaust your staff, lose some of your political capital—all which inevitably leads to a loss of joy for the job. This is why managing yourself in this role is critical (more on that in chapter 6).

Finally, it's important to remember that, regardless of the crisis you are facing, you must continue to focus on your long-term goals. Given the challenges higher education faces today, it is easy to spend all of your time putting out fires. However, if you do so without simultaneously moving forward your long-term strategic goals, you will not be successful in your role. Your job is to never lose sight of the goals, and despite the challenges you face along the way, always redirect your team toward the vision.

Advice from the Deans

On Leading in Crisis

Every dean I interviewed has experienced crisis management firsthand. Although they all mention their response depends on individual situations, they all agree that relying on various tactics is always a winning strategy. These include forming strong relationships prior to the crisis, detaching from your emotions, and forming support networks.

> "In a crisis," I often ask, "What can change do for you, versus to you?" Often a crisis is about something that is changing, and people often feel victimized by it, but I try to remind my constituents, is there a way we can view this as an opportunity? I also try to remain human. Often leaders hold back any emotion. While not oversharing, I always remind my teams during crisis that I too am human, that the situation is impacting me deeply, and that we are all in it together.
>
> —Kasey Urquidez, former vice president, enrollment management and dean, admissions, University of Arizona[27]

> Presence of mind is often so difficult to maintain in the hottest of moments, but it's so important. It's recognizing that in every stimulus-response moment, there's that little space, the dash, between stimulus and response. Your job is to make that dash as long a hyphen as possible.
>
> —Ken Anselment, former vice president for enrollment and communication, Lawrence University[28]

> What got me through several crises in this role were having a strong relationship with my bosses (knowing they would always have my back), reminding myself that this job is not my entire life, and most importantly, practicing self-care. If I don't take care of myself first, nothing else matters.
>
> —Joseph "J. T." Duck, dean of admissions, Tufts University[29]

> Have people in your life, outside of work, that you can lean on and can support you. There is so much that you won't be able to share with your teams. It will get hard. But when you have a support network outside of work, it makes handling the difficult things at work more manageable.
>
> —Whitney Soule, vice provost and dean of admissions, University of Pennsylvania[30]

In times of crisis I use two words intentionally: for and with. I am here for you, and I am here with you. It means that you are supporting my teams and community, and I am also willing to walk side by side with them on this journey. In times of crisis words matter, and you should choose them intentionally. Let people know you have their back. It almost always brings down the temperature.

—Mark Steinlage, vice president of enrollment management, Rockhurst University[31]

In a crisis, I always ask myself—am I going to care about this in five years? This question always gives me perspective and reminds me that no matter how challenging the situation, this moment will pass.

—Satyajit Dattagupta, executive vice chancellor, chief enrollment officer, and senior advisor to the president, Northeastern University[32]

Always have hard conversations in person. I believe that it's really hard to hate up close, which is why tense conversations must happen in person. Email, texts, and messages are never going to solve your challenges. You must do the hard work in person. It almost always brings down the temperature, and mitigates misunderstanding. At a minimum, it also shows that you respect people enough to show up for them, in person.

—Mark Steinlage, vice president of enrollment management, Rockhurst University[33]

There are seldom emergencies in our business, and not every problem is a crisis, despite the tendency of some people to magnify and vocalize things that way. Henry Kissinger once said that university politics were so petty precisely because the stakes were so small. You almost always have time to deal with situations that arise; try not to act in haste, but rather take a deep breath, go for a walk, or sleep on things, and you'll almost always find balance and perspective that come with time.

—Jon Boeckenstedt, vice provost of enrollment management, Oregon State University[34]

CHAPTER 6

Self-Management

The hardest person you will ever lead is yourself.
—Bill George and Peter Sims, *True North*

This is the chapter I wish someone had written for me years ago. Becoming a dean of admission can lead to immense joy, meaning, and purpose, but if you don't approach the job strategically by learning to manage yourself, it can lead to burnout and even resentment. The truth is, you are a precious resource. If you do not engage in practices to ensure you are well cared for, you will be unable to go for the long haul.

In both of my deanships, I made the terrible mistake of allowing the job to take over my life. I was "all in." Although this practice led to incredible success for the colleges I worked for, it also led to incredible sacrifices to my health and personal life. I set few boundaries and pretty soon found myself burned out, twenty pounds overweight, and constantly riddled with stress. I missed important life events—friends' weddings, birthdays, births, and others—because the job always came first. I would work for months at a time, often without a day off, collapse, and then do it all over again. I was caught in a vicious cycle and couldn't see the forest for the trees. In fact, I once went for my annual physical, and my doctor told me, "You're going to have to learn to control the job, not let the job control you—or else you'll die at an early age."

Many deans of admission have confidentially shared with me they too have made incredible sacrifices for the job. One told me he had a heart attack, another told me she suffered incredible panic attacks, whereas several others told me their personal lives had suffered tremendously; divorces and breakups were typical.

Most of us would think a doctor telling us we are unwell would be a wake-up call, but often, we just keep going. I didn't listen to my doctor's warning. I became NACAC CEO and continued to function the way I always did. I allowed the job to take over my entire life, and this time, the challenges were even more intense—given the pandemic, financial challenges, and organizational change I wrote about in the previous chapters. Although I was certainly making a difference in the organization, my own body and mental strength were deteriorating. It wasn't until a serious episode with burnout that I realized something had to change. If you google "executive burnout" and my name, you will find an article I wrote for the American Society of Association Executives about it.[1] This article went viral in both the college access and association spaces. Hundreds of people wrote to me to share their stories and to tell me they too had experienced significant burnout. I then decided to do a podcast about it with Ethan Sawyer (the College Essay Guy), and within a few days, it had several thousand downloads.[2] It's clear that my experience was similar to that of many of my colleagues, and I was not alone. I began to realize part of preparing leaders for these positions meant helping them find ways to manage themselves.

Leaders must engage in practices that are going to help them sustain productivity for the long haul. These include managing energy, having a strategy for when to say "no," being strategic about making room in your life for joy, creating daily routines, and making time to be alone, in silence. These are a few of the strategies I will highlight in this chapter.

I realize now that without intentional management, burnout is typical in the admission deanship. I am reminded of a powerful quote I read during my own burnout phase from restaurateur David Chang. In his memoir, he writes, "Recovering alcoholics talk about needing to hit rock bottom before they are able to climb out. The paradox for the workaholic is that rock bottom is the top of whatever profession they are in."[3] That quote hit me like a ton of bricks—it resonated so deeply with my own experience as a dean.

I am grateful for that time in my life, because I have made significant changes since. I no longer aim for work-life balance: I am for work-life integration. What that means is I accept my work demands are not going to happen neatly between traditional work hours, so I have to find ways to integrate the other important parts of my life into my routine. For years, I wrestled with the question, how do I work hard at a job I love AND continue to do the things that bring me joy, health, and rest?

If you accept a deanship (or any leadership role for that matter), you have to realize the job does not happen during the hours of 9 a.m. to 5 p.m., Monday through Friday. If you want to live a joyful, robust life as a leader and make time for the things you care about most, you must shift your mindset from the pursuit of work-life balance to work-life integration. We live in an age where leaders are called upon to be responsive to issues around the clock. There are times when leaders can get the job done during regular business hours, but the truth is, it's increasingly rare—especially for deans, who often work on campuses where evening and weekend responsibilities are par for the course—and a crisis can arise at any minute. The question to ask yourself is: How can I create a system that allows me to be fully present for my work duties and builds guardrails that protect my personal time, energy, and health? The answer to that question is different for every individual, but I'd like to offer guidance on how to get started.

In this chapter, I describe the practices that have worked for me. By no means do I suggest doing each of these exactly as I describe will work for you—we are all different, and what works for one does not work for another. However, I suggest you use these as motivators to create your own list of self-management strategies. Create the list and keep it somewhere close. When the going gets tough (and it will), you'll need a constant reminder to do what flight attendants remind us every time we fly: put on your own mask first before helping others.

KEY STRATEGIES FOR SUCCESS

Manage Your Energy, Not Your Time

For years, I thought if I had the perfect calendar, I would find ways to thrive. If my calendar had commitments from 9 a.m. to 5 p.m. on the weekdays with few commitments on the weekends, that would help me stay balanced. Well, the harsh realities of serving in leadership roles showed me this approach was unrealistic. Any leadership role you take on does not transpire neatly between the hours of 9 a.m. and 5 p.m.—especially not roles in higher education. There are many evening commitments, tons of travel, weekend board meetings, and emergencies that must be attended to after hours. I still remember how often the student government would summon me at 9 p.m. on Sundays to share their concerns or invite me into a policy discussion.

After many years of struggling to manage my time, I realized I was approaching it the wrong way. For me to show up to the job with energy and enthusiasm, I needed to learn how to manage my energy. This means having a clear understanding of what consumes my energy and what replenishes it. My job (with the help of my scheduling assistant) was to figure out where to put strategic pauses in my calendar and to balance my time between the things that bring me energy and those that deplete it. It is also important to build clear boundaries about what sacrifices I am not willing to make.

At NACAC, I sit with my assistant at the start of each year to create a strategy for my calendar. There are periods when we can predict I will be running out of steam. We put intentional pauses on the calendar, including recovery days. One of the gravest mistakes I used to make was filling up my calendar to the brim. I used to believe the more I did, the more impactful I would be. For me, exhaustion also leads to crankiness. I tend to be a glass-half-full, joyful person. But when I'm exhausted, everything feels negative to me, and that's when my decision-making suffers. I now realize the more I take time to intentionally pause, the more physical energy and mental clarity I have to do the work. Research has shown exhaustion leads to poor decision-making—and one of the most important jobs you will have as a leader is to make tough decisions.[4] To have mental clarity, you must have energy—and that starts by protecting time on your calendar. If you fill your calendar, you're not leaving space for the emergencies and last-minute urgent matters that will inevitably come up.

Finally, take time to understand what activities give you energy, and make sure you include those in your calendar as well. When I was an admission dean, my assistant knew mentoring students gave me energy. Meeting with them on a regular basis reminded me of why I did the work in the first place. During the weeks I had difficult, or "energy-sucking," meetings, she would insert mentorship meetings with my students. It never failed: each time I met with them, I left the meeting feeling energized and joyful. It's also one of the reasons that, despite my busy schedule, I agreed to teach courses on campus. My assistant always thought

I was crazy for adding teaching to an already full schedule, but to me, there was no greater high than watching students learn and grow in the classroom. Teaching re-energized me and reminded me of why I did the work.

Over the years, I also learned that intellectual exercises gave me tons of energy. I loved writing, reading, and researching topics about higher education. These activities can help balance out the routine, but necessary responsibilities deplete your energy. This is why, in all of my jobs, I have dedicated time to writing articles, opinion pieces, and now this book. I sometimes hold a few hours on my calendar to research a topic deeply or read a leadership book that is going to help me strengthen my organization. All these things bring me great joy and recharge my batteries. If you had a few extra hours on your calendar, how would you use them to bring you energy?

It's also just as important to understand what depletes your energy. For me, energy zappers are budget meetings, I.T. conversations, and annual audits conducted by financial firms. Make sure you don't schedule energy-sucking events back to back, or even on a weekly basis. Doing so may mean putting yourself at risk of burnout. Think of your schedule as a roller coaster ride: to get through the lows (energy-depleting activities), you must also schedule the highs (those activities that bring you great joy).

Remember, your schedule is yours to shape. Although the deanship comes with many commitments, it also offers an incredible amount of flexibility to design a schedule that works for you. So, take time to define your guardrails and put them into action. One that has worked for me is no meetings before 10 a.m. I like to get to my office around 9 a.m. and have at least an hour to walk around, catch up with my team, read materials for upcoming meetings, and so on. It allows me to start the day at my pace. It also allows me to do one of the things that brings me great energy and joy—connect with my colleagues.

Learn to Say "NO"

One of the greatest acts of self-care is to say "no." This is incredibly difficult in the college admission counseling profession. In my experience, we are a "yes" profession. We are trained to please as many people as possible and to not let opportunities pass us by. For many years, I suffered from what Oprah Winfrey calls the "disease to please."[5] I rarely said no, which meant I was always overcommitted

Design Thinking Exercise for Energy Management

I used to teach a course titled "Designing Your Life," the content of which was created by Stanford Design School lecturers Bill Barnett and Dave Evans.[6] I had the privilege of being a part of their first higher education cohort, which trained educators on this transformative curriculum (at the time, this was the most popular course at Stanford University). One of the exercises I used to share with my students often helped them understand what gave them energy and what depleted their energy—and what they should try to do more of to maintain a balance. I highly recommend this exercise as you consider your own energy management.

> For a few weeks, keep a list of every activity you take part in. Write down your activities from the moment you wake up until you go to bed—from exercise, to reading, spending time with your kids, budget meetings, financial aid meetings, time with students, and more. At the end of each day, in one column, write next to each item whether you feel it gave you energy or depleted your energy—did it help propel you to the next item in your day, or did it slow you down, leaving you wanting a break? Then, in the next column, write whether you felt engaged and fully present in the activity or just tried to get through it.
>
> At the end of the few weeks, go back through your journal and try to make connections. What depletes your energy and what feeds you? What are some of the activities you engage in where time passes and you barely notice (a "flow state")? What are some of the trends you are seeing? Your goal should be to balance the activities that deplete your energy with those that invigorate you. Do more activities that put you in flow, and you will be energized by the job for a long time.[7] I find that doing this exercise once a year is very helpful because our responsibilities change over time, and so do our responses to them.

and exhausted. I once worked a full day at my job in Los Angeles and then took a red-eye flight to speak the next day for twenty minutes at an event in New York. I returned that same night to Los Angeles, feeling resentful and exhausted as I prepared for another event the following day. I lost time, energy, and productivity for an event I didn't want to or need to attend.

In this profession, there are so many opportunities to say "yes." We are invited to more speaking engagements, case studies programs, panels, and college nights than we could possibly manage. Some of these are really important, maybe even critical, to our enrollment strategy. But the reality is, most of them aren't. Your job is to decipher which events are critical and which are not. I now ask myself three questions before I say "yes" to any invitation.

1. **If I say "yes" to this, what am I saying "no" to in my personal life?** Most of the programs we are invited to require travel, evenings or weekends away from home, and so on. Everything you say "yes" to means you are making a personal sacrifice in your own life. By saying "yes," are you missing dinner with your child (again)? Are you skipping the exercise class you committed to this year? Are you adding yet another weekend of work to your schedule? Before you say "yes," be aware of what you will sacrifice in your own life.
2. **What is my intention?** For so many years, I said "yes" because I didn't want people to be disappointed. That red-eye to Los Angeles would have never happened if I had been honest with myself. I just said "yes" because I didn't want the person who invited me to be disappointed. I now dig deep to understand my intention before saying "yes" to any invitation. Perhaps my intention is to support a good cause or to cultivate a relationship with a school or organization; perhaps it's to help elevate the brand or my organization, or because I would find pure joy in the event. I say "no" a lot more now (although not as much as I should). What I've learned is the people who invite you to do things understand when you say "no," and they move on pretty quickly. So, practice saying "no" more often. It gets easier with time.
3. **Is it a "hell yes"?** In the book *Essentialism*, Greg McKeown paraphrases the popular saying, "If it isn't a hell yes, then it's a hell no."[8] I know it's not always that simple. We often have to do things in our roles that we don't love, but we do them for the good of the institution. However, this question is a great gut check. For example, I once was asked to serve as a trustee at a small liberal arts college. Although I was fond of the president and the institution, my initial reaction was to hesitate. I was worried about the time commitment, about being able to give the role the energy I knew the

organization deserved. I asked myself about my intention. I checked in with my gut and felt a tremendous amount of anxiety about taking on the role. That's when I realized I wasn't yelling, "Hell yes!" at this opportunity. It took me a while to make a decision, but I finally said "no."

Saying "no" is the greatest act of self-care. By saying "no," you dedicate time to things that matter most. It also allows you to focus more deeply on the work projects that will have the greatest impact. Each time I'm tempted to add more to my plate, I remind myself of Steve Jobs's powerful quote: "People think focusing is saying 'yes.' No. Focusing is about saying no."[9]

Now let's discuss some concrete other practices that may allow you to approach work with more energy:

Protect Your Mornings

For years, I would wake up, immediately grab my iPad, and start working. I felt the more I did before I got to the office, the more I could accomplish at work. My mornings consisted of reading the higher ed news so that I could strategize around anything that could affect my institution. I would then answer emails for about an hour, read the global news (which was usually depressing), and try to catch up on projects. The truth is, by the time I got to work, I was already wound up and mentally drained. What I didn't realize then is the way I spent my mornings framed my entire day, and given my routine, I was framing my mornings with negativity. Building a morning routine requires a significant amount of discipline, but it is critical to your success. It means you start the day on your terms, not on the world's agenda. It's incredibly empowering. I know I can't control what happens once I get to my office. By then, we are off to the races. I can control, however, how I start my days and the intentions I set. In his book *Stillness Is the Key*, Ryan Holiday notes: "Order is a prerequisite of excellence and that in an unpredictable world, good habits are a safe haven of certainty. It was Eisenhower who defined freedom as the opportunity for self-discipline. In fact, freedom and power and success require self-discipline. Because without it, chaos and complacency move in. Discipline then, is how we maintain that freedom."[10]

What I've learned over the years is that my mornings are the only time of day I can protect. It is the only time I have to spend in quiet solitude and to frame my intentions for the day. Many leadership experts have written about the importance

Energy Explosion

In his book *The Energy Explosion*, bestselling author Robin Sharma makes five recommendations to keep high levels of energy. These have been incredibly helpful in my own life, and I hope they do the same for you:

1. **Clarity and world-class planning**: Make sure you have clear vision and goals and clarity around what you want to achieve in your life. What is your purpose?
2. **Get up early and do inner work:** Wake up early (the only time of day you actually have control over). Meditate, read, sit in solitude, think, write, or set intentions.
3. **Exercise and diet:** It sounds simple, but many leaders allow this to fall by the wayside. For optimal energy and health, be conscious of how you fuel yourself, and exercise regularly.
4. **Personal renewal:** You must take rest days and recover. You also should work in seasons, which means giving all the energy you have for a specific time period and then pulling back (see more on this in the next section).
5. **Adventure and fun:** Always have something joyous to look forward to.[11]

of creating a morning routine that sets you up for the day, because it's been proven the way you start your day determines the results you achieve.[12]

I now wake up, make coffee, meditate, and read something inspirational. Sometimes the reading is spiritual, when I'm looking for that kind of inspiration. Other times it is leadership oriented, to remind me of how to manage challenging circumstances. Often, I will write in my gratitude journal, a practice I have come to cherish. It helps me start my day with optimism; focused on the positive, instead of the challenges. I find this kind of stillness is now critical for my success. During my reading or meditation, new ideas emerge, and often the answers to the challenges I was looking to solve immediately appear. I now attribute a lot of my current success to stillness. Our world is noisy, and most of us will do anything we can to avoid being alone and sitting quietly—after all, electronic devices are everywhere, tempting us with distraction. However, what I now know for sure is that if you want to be on top of your game, you must find time to sit in stillness.

Each morning, I also do some kind of workout. My goal is to sweat every day. Research has also proven the extraordinary benefits of exercise for your mental and physical health. The endorphins you produce lead to mental clarity, improved moods, decreased levels of stress, and more.[13] I find without exercise I feel sluggish and can't perform at my best. I prefer exercise I can do alone (like swimming and running) because it's another form of meditation. I find the answers I've been seeking about a challenge usually come to me while I'm exercising alone.

These are some of the morning practices that allow me to sustain energy throughout the day. My goal here is not for you to cut and paste but, rather, for you to find what works for you. One of my colleagues, Fanta Aw, CEO of NAFSA (and former vice president for undergraduate enrollment at American University) walks five miles every morning, rain or shine, regardless of where she is in the world. Other friends wake up early to spend time with their young children, because that is what energizes them and brings them the most joy. One of my board members, Chris Loo of the Stonybrook School in New York, sits quietly each morning and prays. Find what works for you, because if you are going to take on challenging roles at work, you are going to need time to prepare your body and mind for the kind of difficulties you will face. Picking up your phone and diving into email, news, or social media first thing in the morning is sure to deplete your energy, but creating a routine that nourishes you will help ensure you perform at your peak.

Limit Your Inputs

Let's face it: we live in a noisy world that's only going to get noisier. What I've learned over the years is if I don't figure out ways to protect how much information I take in, my levels of anxiety will be high. Ryan Holiday writes, "It is difficult to think clearly in rooms filled with other people. It is difficult to understand yourself if you are never by yourself. It's difficult to have much in the way of clarity and insight if your life is a constant party and your home is a construction site. Sometimes, you have to disconnect in order to better connect with yourself and with the people you serve and love."[14]

Over the past several years, I have turned off all notifications on my smartwatch, phone, and other devices. It's amazing how distracting it is to live a life where you are constantly pinging. One of the biggest game-changers for me has been turning off news notifications and changing the way I consume the news. It's important to stay informed about what is happening in the world, but if you don't build guardrails around how and when you consume the news, your energy is guaranteed to be depleted, and your anxiety levels will rise. In fact, research shows our addiction to electronic devices, media, and other sources of constant engagement is hurting us.[15]

I no longer subscribe to news notifications. I allow myself a little time in the morning and a little time in the evening to engage with the news. What's incredible is that, despite not ingesting news throughout the day, I am no less informed about what's happening in the world, but I'm better to focus more on the tasks of my day and worry less about the doom and gloom I often feel after reading news. The key to your success is not about how much information you consume, but rather, what kind of information you allow in.

Another game-changer for me has been to put my phone on "Do Not Disturb" mode. It's a simple tool that not enough people take advantage of. No one says you have to be available all of the time. If you miss a call, you can always return it later. If you are anxious about missing a call from your boss or family, you can program your phone to allow only those notifications to come through. I now keep my phone on "Do Not Disturb" mode most of the time. I choose when to engage. I encourage you to do the same. It's incredibly freeing.

Find Solitude

I have become a strong believer in the use of silence and solitude as a strategic tool for leaders. Robin Sharma writes, "You can't do your part to lead the world to a brighter place if you're always in it."[16]

Another version of limiting your inputs is to spend time alone. This is counterintuitive to most deans, since the position is incredibly outward facing and requires being surrounded by hundreds, sometimes thousands, of people. In fact, four-star General and former Secretary of Defense James Mattis says, "If I was to sum up the single biggest problem of senior leadership in the information age, it's a lack of reflection. Solitude allows you to reflect while other people are reacting.

We need solitude to refocus on prospective decision making, rather than just reacting to problems as they arise."[17] What I've learned over the years is leaders who don't set time aside to think will constantly function on autopilot and make increasingly poor decisions. You might feel that, as an admission dean, the notion of solitude is counterproductive to your role. It's so fast-paced, people oriented, and results driven. Yet, if you don't take the time to step back and sit in silence to make room for your inner voice to emerge, you will spend your time in the role reacting toward the things that come toward you, instead of being intentional about how you want to lead.

I try to sit in solitude on a regular basis, especially now that I serve as NACAC CEO. I am constantly surrounded by people, sometimes thousands of them—at conferences, speaking engagements, airports, and more. I consider myself an extrovert, so I genuinely enjoy the company, but I now realize that engaging in silence is how I make good decisions and problem solve. Silence provides clarity. Silence is part of the morning routine I described—meditating for twenty minutes, engaging in solo exercise. When I am silent, I'm better able to make connections, think of the big picture, and find the answers I've been looking for. This isn't a new concept; in fact, many philosophers and religious traditions throughout history have promoted the transformative power of silence. Robert L. Smith, the former head of school at Sidwell Friends, a Quaker School in Washington, D.C., notes, "Wisdom begins in silence. Quakers believe that only when we have silenced our voices and our souls can we hear the 'still small voice' that dwells within each of us."[18]

In fact, for the past several years, I have made it a priority to embrace longer periods of solitude. I sometimes go on a multi-day solo hike. Other times, I will attend a meditation retreat. Some weekends I will go on a digital detox and spend time at home, alone. When I don't have a lot of time, solitude means going on a run by myself to think—no headphones, no phone, nothing. I am in awe of how the answers to some of the challenges I am facing come naturally to me when I embrace silence and solitude. It not only improves my decision-making and helps me solve complex challenges, but it also helps me become a calmer, more centered leader. Solitude is my recovery time. Citing 2020 research, the Atlantic columnist Arthur Brooks affirms this in his popular column, "How to Build a Life": "The main benefits of solitude noted in the study include contemplation (time to

Silence has helped me navigate very difficult situations throughout my career. The weeks following October 7, 2023, the day Israel suffered a horrific attack and hostages were taken prisoners, I was under extraordinary pressure from many NACAC members across the world to make a statement condemning the attacks. It was a painful experience for me, since many of the people asking for me to make a statement were longtime friends and colleagues. I did not want them to feel I did not care about the pain they (and their students) were experiencing. Yet I knew that making a statement could have very serious implications for the organization. It also had the possibility of creating very serious divisions among the membership. Despite how much pressure I was getting to respond immediately, I decided to sit in silence instead. For days, I sat in meditation each morning, and I dedicated one Saturday to sitting in absolute silence (no phones, devices, television, and so on).

The answer became clear to me. I would reach out to every single person that reached out to me. I would host listening sessions to listen and learn with intent and to understand their perspectives. I wanted to meet with our Jewish Special Interest Group and visit with them in person at our national conference that year. I would also invite my board and leadership team into a conversation about the situation and ask for their best counsel. Although it was certainly time consuming, it was this type of inclusive leadership I felt the moment required. I learned a lot from those listening sessions, and often the conversations were heart wrenching. In the end, I did not make a statement, which some of my members understood, and others are still disappointed about. However, every single person I engaged told me they felt heard, appreciated that I listened, and that I showed up. Without the time I took to sit in stillness, I'm not sure I would have been as intentional about how I addressed this issue.

think, ponder, or reflect); enjoyable solo activities such as reading; mental repose; autonomy; contentment in peace and quiet; and the ability to focus."[19]

Another study, from 2017, showed solitude lowers high levels of emotional affect—turbulent moods, in ordinary parlance—and can lead to relaxation and lower stress. In other words, "being by yourself is a great way to calm down when you feel overstimulated."[20]

If you are not used to spending time alone, start small. Spend a weekend morning with no devices (this includes television) and with no other people. Then try it for an entire day. Once you feel the benefits, you may want to go for a weekend, or an entire week.

And speaking of recovery time, you must take time off. It's nonnegotiable. It sounds obvious and overly simplistic to write this in a book about leadership; however, you'd be surprised how many deans go months without taking time. I know, because I was one of them. I would often go for many months without taking vacation. My mindset was that the academic year started in August and ended in May or June—so until everything was done, I could not rest. You can imagine how gobsmacked I was when I read this quote by Buddhist teacher Frank Ostaseki: "We often think of rest as something that will come to us when everything else in our lives is complete: at the end of the day, when we take a bath; once we go on holiday or get through all our to do lists. We imagine that we can only find rest by changing our circumstances."[21]

The truth is—the work of being a dean is never done, so you have to put intentional pauses in your year to make it through the long haul.

Taking time off to recuperate and rejuvenate isn't just important for you, it's critical for the people you lead. What message are you sending to your teams when you run yourself into the ground? As a leader, people are always watching, and whether it's intentional, not taking time away means others feel they shouldn't either. This is especially true for more junior team members, as well as women, who often feel more pressure and expectations from their work than men. The former president of Wellesley College, Diane Chapman Walsh, reminds us of this in her book, *The Claims of a Life*:

> Is it possible to lead well without taking time out regularly to renew and replenish, read and reflect? And if we believe we can remain effective with no time for . . . wholeness, we are still left with the question of what sort of message we want to convey to younger women. By assuming the mantle of leadership, we've

> traded glass ceilings for glass houses into which everyone can peer for a glimpse of how it's truly going for you in there as we blaze new trails, but equally who we are being in these demanding, competitive, crazy lives that we've chosen or had thrust upon us. It matters because, as we used to taunt LBJ in our youth, "The whole world is watching."[22]

Work in Seasons

When planning your annual schedule, I invite you to follow the good advice of author Cal Newport. In his book *Slow Productivity: The Lost Art of Accomplishment Without Burnout*, he invites us to work in seasons. He argues our bodies require change, and it's unhealthy to work at the same pace all the time (a mistake I made for many, many years). He suggests working in seasons instead. In other words, work intensely for a season and then pull back and take time off to recover.[23] In the world of college admission, we often believe we can't take a break until the end of the academic year, or until the class has been enrolled. That is the fastest approach to burnout. I now follow Cal Newport's good counsel. There are certain times of year in which I am going a hundred miles an hour, but then I pull back. I hold time on my calendar for time off or to have fewer meetings, or not to travel. I block entire days on my calendar with no meetings. This time is restorative, and it often gives me the fuel and new ideas to approach the next intense season with excitement. Although every dean's season is going to differ, it's important you identify those times throughout the year when you can step away or work at a slower pace. Perhaps it's extending time periods when the college is closed, extending the holiday office closure, or finding time in the summer when you empower others on your team to take the lead and for you to step away from the day-to-day schedule. I challenge you to experiment with the idea of working in seasons. Start small. Block out a few days on your calendar, and instead of having meetings all day, work from somewhere else (not your office) and dig into creative projects, strategy, or planning. I assure you that both you and your institution will be stronger for it.

Build Guardrails

When you become a dean, the demands on your time can feel relentless. Your day-to-day schedule is filled with meetings, campus events, travel, speaking engagements, media engagement, staff management, and much more. For your days to be sustainable, you must learn to build guardrails. Some of this certainly means learning to say "no," as discussed earlier in this chapter. But it also means understanding what your non-negotiables are. For example, for some deans with children, this may mean not missing their children's sports or recitals. For others, it may mean not working several weekends in a row or being on the road for more than a few days at a time. Early in your deanship, you must figure out what your guardrails are, because if you don't, the position will take over your entire life. As I mentioned, one of my guardrails has always been that I don't want to be scheduled for meetings very early in the morning. Mornings are often my time to think, prepare, read, write, and catch up. If I give away this precious time, I find myself off-kilter. I also try not to go on work trips that last more than one week. Although it's not always possible, it's good to have the guardrail in place. I find that as I get older, the life of a road warrior affects the body differently, and in an effort to stay energized and able to perform at my best, I try to give myself recovery time between trips—especially if they require significant time zone changes or many late-night events.

Find Your Support Network

Finally, it's important to find a close network of friends and family you can confide in to discuss the highs and lows of your work. The deanship is a lonely role. Before you became a dean, you had peers whom you could talk to, perhaps even gossip and commiserate with. That all stops the minute you become a dean. When I became a dean, I had to be careful about what I shared with my staff, and as noted earlier in this book, my job was to lead with optimism. But it didn't mean I should hold all of my emotions in. I just needed to find a different network and support, because I shouldn't rely on my staff or other members of the college community to validate my feelings.

I still remember the day I was having one of my weekly meetings with my boss, the president of the college. I was sharing a difficult meeting I had with several athletic coaches and faculty members and my feelings of how they were rude and borderline hostile. I was feeling sorry for myself and wondering why these members of the college community didn't care about my feelings. She allowed me to go on for a few minutes. Then she leaned across the table and put her hand over mine, and with the gentlest tone said, "When leaders want sympathy, they should get a puppy."

I couldn't help but smile because I understood exactly what she meant. As leaders, you can't look for validation or sympathy in the environment in which you lead. You represent a role that most people come to you to share their emotions. You are there to help solve their issues. However, although I don't believe it's intentional, most people will not consider how their actions make you feel. This was one of the big paradigm shifts I had to make when I became a dean. However, it does not mean leaders aren't human. Form a network of people you can talk to about your most challenging moments. It could be a colleague on another campus, a mentor, close friends, or a spouse. As a dean, I actually worked with an executive coach and still do to this day. I highly recommend it, because there's nothing like having a neutral party to talk to when the going gets tough—and it will get tough.

Executive Coaching

The practice of seeking executive coaching has become increasingly popular, reflecting a broader workplace trend of doing personal work to cultivate a culture of improvement and adaptability. One of the most transformative experiences of my career has been to work with an executive coach. I have been fortunate to work with several, and I highly recommend that you, too, work with a trusted coach. Given that it's "lonely at the top," this is someone you can process challenges with, run ideas by, and get leadership advice from. Working with a coach is an opportunity to step away from the demands and the noise of the role to focus solely on yourself, your goals, and your development. The best coaches don't give you the answers—rather, they ask you the right questions so that you can get to the answers yourself. They help you find perspective and provide you with leadership tools that help you grow. It's important you find a coach you feel comfortable with and with whom you can develop a great rapport. Many presidents and provosts are willing to provide a coach as part of the dean's compensation package, but even if they don't, I suggest you invest in yourself and hire one. There is no greater investment in your professional development than working with a coach.

Because it's so important, I will end the chapter the same way I started it: "The hardest person you will ever have to lead is yourself." Without a clear sense of who you are—your own values, motivations, and boundaries—the deanship can overtake your life and threaten your health, relationships, and more. The more you work on self-management, the happier you will be in the role, and the greater success you will have. In my experience, leaders who spend time learning to manage themselves have stronger impact, and they also have a more positive effects on their teams.

Unfortunately, I have also witnessed too many deans creating toxic cultures in the workplace because they themselves are unhappy and dealing with internal unresolved issues. You can't show up to work and give your best when your internal life is in upheaval. Ashley Perzyna, chief operating officer at NACAC and one of my great thought partners on self-management, says it best: "A leader should not create a storm in others when they are dealing with a storm inside of themselves."[24] I meet so many people in the profession who tell me they are leaving their offices because they work in a toxic culture, often because of a challenging supervisor. They are disillusioned by the micromanagement, unrealistic work hours, a lack of psychological safety, and more. It makes me incredibly sad because I want good people to stay and grow in the field. So often they leave not because they didn't enjoy the work but because they are working for leaders who haven't learned to manage themselves and are unintentionally creating storms in the workplace.

Self-management is a skill. It can be learned and honed. And I implore you, once you do, teach the skill to others. Imagine a college admission profession where leaders across the globe are performing at their best and having an incredibly positive impact on their teams and institutions. The results would be transformative.

Advice from the Deans

On Self-Management

Every dean I interviewed admitted that self-management was something they were constantly working on. They each find it really challenging but understand it is critical. Building guardrails, stepping away periodically, and finding ways to build joy into your calendar were some of the most common themes they shared.

> Leaders need to understand that how they manage their own health sets a tone for their team, who will often take their cues for "expected behavior" from the actions of their leaders. "Do what I say; don't do what I do," is not only a cliche, it's disingenuous.
>
> —Ken Anselment, former vice president for enrollment and communication, Lawrence University[25]

> I always have something to look forward to on my calendar. These jobs are so intense, so you must have something joyful to look forward to.
>
> —Kasey Urquidez, former vice president for enrollment management, University of Arizona[26]

> For me, work-life integration is important. For example, I know that I need catch up time every evening, but I protect 5–9 p.m. to be with my wife and child. You have to know what your boundaries are. That's how you can have a robust professional life and nourish your personal life as well.
>
> —Fumio Sugihara, dean of admissions and financial aid, Hampshire College[27]

> You have to figure out what brings you joy and make sure you find time for those things. If you don't have a clear commitment to being a whole human being outside of this role, you won't be able to live a full, joyful life.
>
> —Whitney Soule, vice provost and dean of admissions, University of Pennsylvania[28]

> I've never missed breakfast with my kids on their birthday. No matter where I have to travel to for work, I always fly home for this tradition.
>
> —Kasey Urquidez, former vice president for enrollment management, University of Arizona[29]

> I took off all notifications from my phone so I don't get a notification every time a new work email comes through. I try to be good about not being on email on the weekends.
>
> —Joseph "J. T." Duck, dean of admissions, Tufts University[30]

Just how we have to unplug, you also have to plug into the things that give you energy. Make time for the things that fill your soul.

—Mark Steinlage, vice president of enrollment management, Rockhurst University[31]

One of the ways to create better boundaries between you and the job is by learning to delegate and empower others on your team. So much of the burnout comes from trying to take everything on yourself. Empowering others and delegating allows your team to grow, and gives you the room to do other things, or better yet, take time to recover.

—Johnnie Johnson, vice president for enrollment management, Washington College[32]

I am unwilling to compromise weekends with my family. I will never let work get in the way of precious time with my wife and kids. I love making breakfast for my family, and it brings me great joy. Life is too short to allow the job to get in the way of that.

—Mark Steinlage, vice president of enrollment management, Rockhurst University[33]

Conclusion

> In business, it doesn't matter what you do, it matters why you do it. Steve Jobs, the Wright Brothers and Martin Luther King have one thing in common: they started with "why."
>
> —Simon Sinek, author and speaker

Before I end the book, I think it's time for me to make a heartfelt confession. Although I loved both of my deanships and would absolutely still have become a dean given all that I know now, I also considered quitting several times.

During my first deanship at Pitzer College, I made the mistake of giving the job my all and neglecting many other aspects of my life. To be clear, I loved Pitzer. No school's mission and values have ever resonated with me so deeply. The institution's staunch focus on social responsibility, environmental sustainability, and intercultural understanding was the reason I felt passionate about representing this particular institution. Yet the pace at which I worked started to slowly chip away at my love affair with the college. The competitive nature of the board, president, and faculty at the time also left me feeling defeated. What I found is the exhaustion did not allow me to think clearly, and I began to feel increasingly disillusioned with the job each day.

I still remember attending a meeting where several professors in the STEM fields felt the first-year students they taught needed more preparation in math. "It's time for you to bring us better students," one professor remarked. Another said, "Your job is to bring us the best and the brightest!" At that moment, I didn't practice the intentional pause I usually take before responding and instead immediately replied, "Actually, I believe my job is to bring you the ready, willing and able, and *YOUR* job is to make them the best and the brightest." As you can imagine, my response did not land well. It made me sound defensive, and as a result, their frustration (and complaints) grew.

Right after the meeting with faculty members, I was scheduled to attend my weekly meeting with the president. I was eager to attend this meeting since our agenda was to discuss goals for the following academic year. Despite some of the faculty's issues with first-year math preparation, admission was thriving. We were exceeding our revenue goals, bringing in diverse, academically talented cohorts of students from all over the world, and the admit rate was at a historic low, 13 percent. During our meeting, I asked the president to share her vision for our future. She said, "Next year, we lower the admit rate to at least 12 percent, we decrease the discount rate, and we increase our net tuition revenue." Admittedly, I was having this conversation after a difficult meeting with faculty, and at the end of the academic year, which meant I was already feeling burned out and disillusioned. When she said, "Lower the admit rate and increase net tuition revenue," I had mental flashes of all the grueling work my team and I did over the past year to meet her goals, and the very painful decisions we had to make in admission committee. We were a highly tuition-driven institution, and the trade-offs we had to make in admission committee to meet our revenue goals were painful. I kept thinking, How would I go back and inspire my team toward these new goals? I could already anticipate their disappointment. As these images flashed through my head, I tried not to show frustration at her response, but I did muster the strength to ask her the question: "Why is this the goal? When is it going to be enough?" She made her goal clear and did not budge. I walked away from the meeting and was determined to quit.

The combination of exhaustion and frustration left me feeling numb. Yet, this is where the power of your network is *SO* critical. Fortunately, I had trusting relationships with other deans in the field who could empathize with my experience and help me think objectively. They understood how challenging it was to meet board and trustee goals and how those goals were not always in alignment with the way deans felt the work should be done. Those friendships with other deans made all the difference in reminding me about the trade-offs, that taking the long view was important, and that there was still incredible joy in the work.

I also had family and friends who supported me through the burnout phase. They reminded me I actually did love the job and the institution, that I cared so deeply for that community and its students—but that my approach to the work needed to change. I needed more time for rest and recovery, and I needed to practice more detachment if I were going to thrive in the role. Thankfully, I decided to stay at Pitzer and continued to find great joy in the work. My time there includes some of my fondest professional memories. I didn't realize that, when I eventually moved on to a new institution, the same urge to quit would plague me again.

After a few years as vice president for enrollment and student success, I called the president of Trinity College and said, "I think it's time for me to leave this job. You should hire someone else." She was shocked. In many ways, I was thriving. Although the enrollment landscape was challenging, and the politics within the institution was powerful, I was meeting my goals and moving the institution forward in extraordinary ways. I built a high-performing team and established many strong relationships on campus and beyond. Yet I was starting to wonder if I could do this for the long haul—not because I didn't have the energy, but rather because I wasn't sure I wanted to continue to fight the politics, which felt ever present on that campus. I had also recently become the topic of discussion on a popular Facebook page for parents and alumni. Although most of the comments were based on perception not reality, it created a lot of noise and distraction on campus and left me feeling mentally drained. Situations such as these, in addition to a hectic work pace, can often make you feel doubtful. At that moment, I wasn't sure if I wanted to shepherd another crisis or wake up on another May 1 wondering if I would have a job on May 2. To be fair, I don't believe the president would've fired me if I missed the enrollment target (she was incredibly supportive), but my responsibilities weighed heavily on me. Knowing that missing the target could impact the finances of the entire institution kept me up at night. Would I be able to withstand the backlash that would ensue in the community if I didn't meet my enrollment goals? Every year, I thought about the irony of my job and the fact that being an admission dean was such volatile work. I would ask myself the same question: "Are you sure you want to stay in a job where your success depends on the whims of seventeen-year-olds?" I certainly was not alone. These are emotions most admission deans feel on a regular basis.

What happened after I told the president I might quit reaffirms my belief that whom you work for matters deeply. How they coach, mentor, and support you can be the difference between staying and thriving, and crashing and burning. Despite her surprise, the president of Trinity's response was kind, gentle, and strategic—three attributes that have always defined her leadership.

I'm delighted to say that, even after my sudden and potentially final phone call to the president, I stayed in the position. What was her encouragement? "Before you make a rash decision, you should reconnect with your 'why.'" Like others in the past, she encouraged me to take the long view. "In leadership, there will always be difficult moments," she told me. "That's when it's most important to reconnect to why you decided to begin this leadership journey in the first place, and to remind yourself of what you want success to look like down the road." I took that counsel very seriously. I decided to spend time in solitude and also journal about why I got into this work in the first place. I also took a few long weekends off—something I hadn't done in a long time.

As I sat in quiet reflection, I remembered the high school counselor and admissions officer who changed my life. I reflected on the thousands of students whose journeys to and through college I was fortunate to support. I smiled as I wrote in my journal about the rock star teams I had built, and how much I enjoyed working with, and cultivating, them. I also thought about the fiscal health of the institutions I served and how my work in managing net tuition revenue was a significant factor in allowing the institution to deliver on its mission. My work helped make it possible for these institutions to thrive.

I also sat with the hundreds of handwritten and emailed thank you notes I've received over the years (I keep as many as possible). Some were from students, who came from all over the world and thanked me for changing their lives, as many came from low-income backgrounds and could never have afforded their education without our generous financial aid funding. Some were from staff members who had moved on to leadership roles and were grateful for my guidance. Some were from high school counselors who were thankful for me taking a chance on one of their students—who now couldn't be happier in college. Some were from former students who took my classes and said, "Your class changed my perspective," and finally, some were from trustees who wrote to say, "Thank you for taking such good care of my college.'"

I still joke with friends that being an admission dean is "the toughest job you'll ever love," a phrase often used to describe the Peace Corps.[1] But I'm so glad I decided to stay in my deanships. As I reflect on my time on those two campuses, they were some of the most challenging and joyous growth opportunities of my life. What I couldn't appreciate then is that the difficult moments in those roles were gradually shaping my growth as a leader and preparing me for more. I don't believe I would be as effective in my role as NACAC CEO without those experiences. I am a stronger storyteller, politician, crisis manager, supervisor, and mentor because of those deanships. If you stay and grow in your role, I believe you will be, too.

It's amazing what happens when you take time to reflect and reconnect with your "why." The challenges start to fade away into the background. To this day, I make it a priority to regularly reconnect with my "why," especially on the days when I feel like my job is most challenging. I still keep those thank you cards and gracious emails, but I also keep a gratitude journal. Each week, I sit down and write about good things that happened at work (and in my personal life). Sometimes it's something someone said to me, a goal I've met, or impact I've made. I sit down to review my journal often, because I find that it's difficult to be cranky or stressed when you reflect on gratitude. In fact, most of the research published on gratitude shows a positive correlation between gratitude and well-being.

During my interviews with deans for this book, many affirmed what has kept them in the work is their individual passion for it. Each of them has a deeply personal reason for entering the profession and staying in it. In fact, Satyajit at Northeastern told me he intentionally reconnects with his "why" each year. "Everyone talks about how stressful these jobs are," he said. "Sure they are, but so are many other jobs. In these roles, we get to change the lives of hundreds of thousands of students. I'm so fortunate!"[2]

Finally, I want to share a strategy that has sustained me throughout all of my leadership roles, especially my current one: If you reframe challenge into opportunity, you will approach every issue you face with a very different mindset.

In his book *The Obstacle Is the Way*, Ryan Holiday writes, "The obstacle in the path becomes the path. Never forget, within every obstacle is an opportunity to improve our condition."[3] This is why in all my leadership roles, and especially now as NACAC CEO, I have asked myself this question when presented with difficult situations:

"*What is this moment supposed to teach me?*"

Every time I am facing a crisis or a challenge that feels overwhelming, I pause and seek the answer to this question. The answer doesn't always surface immediately; in fact, it often it takes time and distance to be able to see the situation clearly. However, the lesson always arrives. And what happens in the meantime is powerful. Instead of complaining or dreading that something is happening *to ME*, I approach the situation with greater curiosity and optimism, rather than dread or frustration. I almost look forward to the challenge, because I can't wait to see what I'm meant to learn from it, to experience how much stronger I might become.

What I've now come to understand is every single one of the challenges I faced as a dean was a step toward greater resiliency and stronger leadership.

When I first arrived at NACAC, my staff would remark at how calm I was, despite the challenges we were facing and the sensitive politics we were navigating. I didn't realize it then, but the reason I was able to approach each situation with relative calm was I had toned the mental muscles I needed to thrive in my leadership roles as a dean. Although I certainly continue to face challenging moments as CEO, very little surprises me anymore, and when something does, I approach it using all the tools I have shared with you in this book.

There will be no shortage of challenging issues that current and future deans of admission will face. As I write the closing of the book, a new presidential administration is entering the White House, one that has made it clear that they will make things more difficult for higher education.[4] The Department of Education staff has been cut in half, and colleges are being sent threatening letters in an effort to dismantle DEI.[5] Skepticism around the value of higher education abounds, and greater interference in admissions work by politicians across the nation will certainly add a layer of complexity to enrollment management. Yet despite all the challenges I have outlined in this book, I remain incredibly optimistic about the future of the profession.

The next generation of admission deans and other leaders in the field are poised to overhaul outdated systems, create new ways of operating, and open the doors wider for students from all over the world to access educational opportunity. They will rise to meet the challenges of the day with greater intentionality and a larger skill set than ever before. Unlike my generation, who were forced to sink or swim in the role, the next one will thrive because they will have better roadmaps, more training, and strategic mentorship. I know that is the work I am committed to leading at the National Association for College Admission Counseling and the impetus for writing this book. I envision a profession that transforms the lives of thousands of people and institutions through intentional leadership—a cohort of deans who learned that managing themselves is the tool that empowers them to lead with integrity, grace, and impact. It is also the secret to remaining in the job for the long haul.

Every dean I interviewed for the book was delighted to share the great joy and personal satisfaction they felt by serving in the role. Each of them felt they were living meaningful and purposeful lives and that despite the challenges, they got their joy from realizing the incredible impact they are able to have on the lives of so many students, staff, and community members. They also remarked on how special the college admission counseling community is. Most of them stayed in the work because they also loved the people in the profession.

If you are a sitting dean, I hope you will stay in the work because we need you now more than ever. If you are considering the deanship, I implore you to give it serious consideration. There is great joy and global impact in this field. I firmly believe that the right deanship can transform your life in ways you couldn't ever imagine.

Onward!

Further Reading

Although the following books were published throughout the last few decades, the lessons you will learn in them are evergreen. These are the books I've gifted the most to new leaders, and you will note I have referred to them often throughout this book. I believe the advice in these books will stand the test of time. I recommend you make these a part of your library as you transition or evolve into any new leadership role.

The First 90 Days: Proven Strategies for Getting Up to Speed Faster and Smarter, Michael D. Watkins[6]

Designing Your Life: How to Build a Well-Lived, Joyful Life, Bill Burnett and Dave Evans[7]

Leading Change, John Kotter[8]

Setting the Table: The Transforming Power of Hospitality in Business, Danny Meyer[9]

Slow Productivity: The Lost Art of Accomplishment Without Burnout, Cal Newport[10]

Stillness is the Key, Ryan Holiday[11]

Humble Inquiry: The Gentle Art of Asking Instead of Telling, Edgar H. Schein and Peter A. Schein[12]

Notes

Foreword

1. Eric Hoover, "The Hottest Seat on Campus," *The Chronicle of Higher Education* (September 15, 2014), https://www.chronicle.com/article/the-hottest-seat-on-campus/?sra=true.

Introduction

1. Roberta Espinoza, *Pivotal Moments: How Educators Can Put All Students on the Path to College* (Harvard Education Press, 2011).
2. Sofoklis Goulas, "Twelve Facts About the Economics of Education," *Brookings* (June 27, 2024), https://www.brookings.edu/articles/twelve-facts-about-the-economics-of-education/.
3. Sarah Bray, Annmarie Caño, and Keith E. Whitfield, "Needed: Leadership Training for Faculty and Academic Staff," *Inside Higher Ed* (November 21, 2019), https://www.insidehighered.com/advice/2019/11/22/importance-cultivating-leadership-skills-among-faculty-and-academic-staff-members.
4. Brian Mitchell, "Higher Education Faces Hurdles in 2024," *Forbes* (February 14, 2024), https://www.forbes.com/councils/forbesbusinesscouncil/2024/02/14/higher-education-faces-hurdles-in-2024/.
5. "Strategic Enrollment Management Planning," The Society for College and University Planning (SCUP), https://www.scup.org/planning-type/strategic-enrollment-management-planning/.
6. Burton A. Weisbrod, Jeffery P. Ballou, and Evelyn D. Asch, *Mission and Money: Understanding the University* (Cambridge University Press, 2010).
7. Satyajit Dattagupta (executive vice chancellor, chief enrollment officer, and senior advisor to the president, Northeastern University) discussion with the author, February 13, 2024.
8. Muriel Poston (former dean of the faculty and vice president for Academic Affairs, Pitzer College) discussion with the author, n.d.
9. Alan Earhart, "Higher Education Managers Beware. The Enrollment Cliff Is Here," LinkedIn (January 16, 2024), https://www.linkedin.com/pulse/higher-education-managers-beware-enrollment-cliff-here-earhart-phd-yebxf/.
10. Glenn C. Altschuler and David Whippman, "Higher Education's Perfect Storm Is Becoming a Tsunami," *The Hill* (November 12, 2023), https://thehill.com/opinion/education/4305142-higher-educations-perfect-storm-is-becoming-a-tsunami/.
11. Nina Totenberg, "Supreme Court Guts Affirmative Action, Effectively Ending Race-Conscious Admissions," *NPR* (June 29, 2023), https://www.npr.org/2023/06/29/1181138066/affirmative-action-supreme-court-decision; Claudine Gay, "Personal News," Harvard Office of the President (January 2, 2024), https://www.harvard.edu/president/news-gay/2024/personal-news/; Scott Bok, "A Message to the Penn Community: Resignation of President Liz Magill," *University of Pennsylvania Almanac* (December 12, 2023), https://almanac.upenn.edu/articles/a-message-to-the-penn-community-resignation-of-president-liz-magill; "Announcement from President Minouche Shafik," Columbia Office of the

President (August 14, 2024), https://president.columbia.edu/news/announcement-president-minouche-shafik.

12. Jon Marcus, "A Looming 'Demographic Cliff': Fewer College Students and Ultimately Fewer Graduates," *NPR* (January 8, 2025), https://www.npr.org/2025/01/08/nx-s1-5246200/demographic-cliff-fewer-college-students-mean-fewer-graduates#:~:text=This%20%22demographic%20cliff%22%20has%20been,for%20Disease%20Control%20and%20Prevention.
13. Andrew Bauld, "Does Anyone Win When Colleges Compete?" *Harvard Graduate School of Education Ed. Magazine* (May 24, 2023), https://www.gse.harvard.edu/ideas/ed-magazine/23/05/does-anyone-win-when-colleges-compete; Mark J. Mitchell, "Tuition: Ability to Pay vs. Willingness to Pay," National Association of Independent Schools (NAIS) (Fall 2022), https://www.nais.org/magazine/independent-school/fall-2022/considering-the-markets-ability-to-pay-versus-its-willingness-to-pay/.
14. Melanie Hanson, "Average Private vs Public College Tuition," Education Data Initiative (August 12, 2024), https://educationdata.org/private-vs-public-college-tuition.
15. Abigail Tierney, "Median Household Income in the United States from 1990 to 2023," *Statista* (September 16, 2024), https://www.statista.com/statistics/200838/median-household-income-in-the-united-states/; Melanie Hanson, "Financial Aid Statistics," Education Data Initiative (May 25, 2024), https://educationdata.org/financial-aid-statistics.
16. Melanie Hanson, "Average Student Loan Debt," Education Data Initiative (August 16, 2024), https://educationdata.org/average-student-loan-debt.
17. Brian Rosenberg, *"Whatever It Is, I'm Against It": Resistance to Change in Higher Education* (Harvard Education Press, 2023), 6–7.
18. Elissa Nadworny, "More Than 1 Million Fewer Students Are in College. Here's How That Impacts the Economy," *NPR* (January 13, 2022), https://www.npr.org/2022/01/13/1072529477/more-than-1-million-fewer-students-are-in-college-the-lowest-enrollment-numbers-.
19. Liam Knox, "First-Year Enrollments Take a Tumble," *Inside Higher Ed* (October 23, 2024), https://www.insidehighered.com/news/admissions/traditional-age/2024/10/23/after-fafsa-issues-steep-drop-first-year-enrollment.
20. Jessica Blake, "American Confidence in Higher Ed Hits Historic Low," *Inside Higher Ed* (July 11, 2023), https://www.insidehighered.com/news/business/financial-health/2023/07/11/american-confidence-higher-ed-hits-historic-low; "Anti—DEI Laws Take Aim at Students of Color and LGBTQ+ Students," *NeaToday* (February 14, 2024), https://www.nea.org/nea-today/all-news-articles/anti-dei-laws-take-aim-students-color-and-lgbtq-students#; Kamaron McNair, "Campus Protests, FAFSA Delays Plagued College Admissions This Year—How It Affects Incoming Students, from College Counselors," *CNBC* (May 8, 2024), https://www.cnbc.com/2024/05/08/campus-protests-fafsa-delays-plague-college-admissions-process.htm; Neal Riley, "Emerson College Says Enrollment Down Significantly After 'Negative' Reaction to Student Protests; Layoffs Planned," *CBS News* (June 19, 2024), https://www.cbsnews.com/boston/news/emerson-college-enrollment-protests-layoffs/.
21. Eric Hoover, "Why Admissions Leaders Are Wearing Down, Burning Out, and Leaving Jobs They Once Loved," *The Chronicle of Higher Education* (April 5, 2023), https://www.chronicle.com/article/a-profession-on-the-edge.
22. Megan Zahneis, "Turnover Is Bad Across Higher Education. It's Even Worse in Admissions," *The Chronicle of Higher Education* (April 18, 2023), https://www.chronicle.com/article/turnover-is-bad-across-higher-ed-its-even-worse-in-admissions.
23. "Admission Officer Job Description," Indeed (January 5, 2025), https://ca.indeed.com/hire/job-description/admission-officer.

24. Earvin "Magic" Johnson, "A Leadership Journey with Earvin 'Magic' Johnson,'" (lecture, National Association for College Admission Counseling Annual Conference, Los Angeles, California, September 26, 2024).
25. Wendy Kilgore, "2023 Chief Enrollment Management Officer: Summary of the AACRAO Career Profile Survey," The American Association of Collegiate Registrars and Admissions Officers (AACRAO) (January 29, 2023), https://www.aacrao.org/research-publications/aacrao-research/2023-chief-enrollment-management-officer-summary-of-the-aacrao-career-profile-survey.

Chapter 1

Epigraph: Whitney Soule (vice provost and dean of admissions, University of Pennsylvania), in discussion with the author, February 13, 2024.

1. Shirley Collado (president emeritus, Ithaca College), in discussion with the author, November 13, 2024.
2. Will Guidara, *Unreasonable Hospitality: The Remarkable Power of Giving People More Than They Expect* (Optimism Press, 2022), 98.
3. Lauren Love, "U-M's Fall Enrollment Makes It State's Largest University," *University Record* (October 2, 2023), https://record.umich.edu/articles/u-ms-fall-enrollment-makes-it-states-largest-university/.
4. Fumio Sugihara dean of admission and financial aid, Hampshire College, in discussion with the author, February 13, 2024.
5. Joseph Montgomery (associate vice provost for enrollment management, North Carolina Agricultural and Technical State College), in discussion with the author, February 13, 2024.
6. Lee Coffin (vice president and dean of admissions and financial aid, Dartmouth College), in discussion with the author, October 31, 2024.
7. Joseph "J. T." Duck (dean of admissions, Tufts University), in discussion with the author, February 13, 2024.
8. Allie Bidwell, "College Presidents Turning Attention to Enrollment Management," National Association of Student Financial Aid Administrators (March 26, 2018), https://www.nasfaa.org/news-item/14736/College_Presidents_Turning_Attention_to_Enrollment_Management.
9. Marjorie Haas (president, Council of Independent Colleges), in discussion with the author, October 1, 2024.
10. Delorean "D. J." Menifee (former vice president for enrollment, marketing, and communications, Bradley University), in discussion with the author, February 21, 2024.
11. John Kroger, "The Toughest Job in the Nation," *Inside Higher Ed* (October 18, 2018), https://www.insidehighered.com/blogs/leadership-higher-education/toughest-job-nation.
12. Jon Boeckenstedt (vice provost of enrollment management, Oregon State University), email message to the author, December 1, 2024.
13. Sugihara, February 13, 2024.
14. Menifee, February 21, 2024.
15. "What Is Financial Aid Optimization?" *Carnegie* (August 23, 2022), https://www.carnegiehighered.com/blog/financial-aid-optimization-and-individualized-aid-strategy/.
16. Montgomery, February 13, 2024.
17. Brian Rosenberg, *"Whatever It Is, I'm Against It": Resistance to Change in Higher Education* (Harvard Education Press, 2023), 95.

18. Kasey Urquidez (former vice president, enrollment management, and dean, admissions, University of Arizona), in discussion with the author, February 27, 2024.
19. Ken Anselment (former vice president for enrollment and communication, Lawrence University), in discussion with the author, December 14, 2024.
20. Duck, February 13, 2024.
21. Urquidez, February 27, 2024.
22. Sugihara, February 13, 2024.
23. Soule, February 13, 2024.
24. Mark Steinlage (vice president for enrollment management, Rockhurst University), in discussion with the author, November 7, 2024.

Chapter 2

1. Lee Coffin (vice president and dean of admissions and financial aid, Dartmouth College), in discussion with the author, October 31, 2024.
2. Joseph "J. T." Duc (dean of admissions, Tufts University), in discussion with the author, February 13, 2024.
3. Edgar H. Schein, *Humble Inquiry: The Gentle Art of Asking Instead of Telling* (Berrett-Koehler Publishers, 2013).
4. Lauren Trombley, in discussion with the author, n.d.
5. Ken Anselment (former vice president for enrollment and communication, Lawrence University), in discussion with the author, December 14, 2024.
6. Michael D. Watkins, *The First 90 Days: Proven Strategies for Getting Up to Speed Faster and Smarter* (Harvard Business Review Press, 2013), 12–14.
7. Danny Meyer, *Setting the Table: The Transforming Power of Hospitality in Business* (Ecco Press, 2008), 92.
8. Attributed to Maya Angelou.
9. Will Guidara, *Unreasonable Hospitality: The Remarkable Power of Giving People More Than They Expect* (Optimism Press, 2022), 19.
10. Duck, February 13, 2024.
11. Delorean "D. J." Menifee (former vice president for enrollment, marketing, and communications, Bradley University), in discussion with the author, February 21, 2024.
12. Kasey Urquidez (former vice president, enrollment management, and dean, admissions, University of Arizona), in discussion with the author, February 27, 2024.
13. Satyajit Dattagupta (executive vice chancellor, chief enrollment officer, senior advisor to the president, Northeastern University), in discussion with the author, February 13, 2024.
14. Joseph Montgomery (associate vice provost for enrollment management, North Carolina Agricultural and Technical State College), in discussion with the author, February 13, 2024.
15. Whitney Soule (vice provost and dean of admissions, University of Pennsylvania), in discussion with the author, February 13, 2024.
16. Fumio Sugihara (dean of admissions and financial aid, Hampshire College), in discussion with the author, February 13, 2024.
17. Meyer, *Setting the Table*, 139.
18. Michael Sandler, "Why College Presidents Struggle During Crises," *Inside Higher Ed* (January 2024), https://www.insidehighered.com/opinion/career-advice/2024/01/03/why-many-presidents-struggle-when-dealing-crises-opinion.
19. Attributed to Peter Schutz.

20. Robert Iger, *The Ride of a Lifetime: Lessons Learned from 15 Years as CEO of the Walt Disney Company* (Random House, 2019), 231.
21. Dattagupta, February 13, 2024.
22. Meyer, *Setting the Table*, 141.
23. Meyer, *Setting the Table*, 142–43.
24. "New Research from CUPA-HR Finds Low Retention Rates Among Admissions Employees in Higher Ed," CUPA-HR (April 25, 2024), https://www.cupahr.org/press-releases/higher-ed-admissions-workforce-04-18-2023/.
25. Tramayne Monaghan, "'Nothing Will Kill a Great Employee Faster Than Watching You Tolerate a Bad One'—Perry Belcher," *Medium* (November 10, 2021), https://medium.com/tramayne/nothing-will-kill-a-great-employee-faster-than-watching-you-tolerate-a-bad-one-perry-belcher-d578efe42390.
26. Alexandra Solomon, interview by Ryan Holiday, posted November 12, 2024, "Using Ancient Wisdom to Solve Modern Problems," *Masterclass video*, chapter 1, 18:30:00, https://www.masterclass.com/series/using-ancient-wisdom-to-solve-modern-problems.
27. Dattagupta, February 13, 2024.
28. Attributed to Peter Drucker.
29. Watkins, *First 90 Days*.
30. Iger, *Ride of a Lifetime*, 228.
31. Jennifer Desjarlais (former dean of admission and financial aid, Wellesley College and principal, Cambridge Hill Partners, Inc.), in discussion with the author, n.d.
32. "Mission vs. Vision vs. Value Statement: What They Are and How to Write Them," Indeed for Employers, n.d., https://www.indeed.com/hire/c/info/mission-vision-value-statement.
33. "Mission & Vision," National Association for College Admission Counseling (NACAC), n.d., https://www.nacacnet.org/who-we-are/mission-vision/.
34. Dattagupta, February 13, 2024.
35. Adele C. Brumfield, vice provost for enrollment management, in discussion with the author, April 18, 2024.
36. Anselment, December 14, 2024.
37. Dattagupta, February 13, 2024.
38. Soule, February 13, 2024.
39. Mark Steinlage (vice president for enrollment management, Rockhurst University), in discussion with the author, November 7, 2024.

Chapter 3

1. Frances X. Frei and Anne Morriss, "Storytelling That Drives Bold Change," *Harvard Business Review* (November 1, 2023), https://hbr.org/2023/11/storytelling-that-drives-bold-change.
2. Lee Coffin (vice president and dean of admissions and financial aid, Dartmouth College), in discussion with the author, October 31, 2024.
3. Ken Anselment (former vice president for enrollment and communication, Lawrence University), in discussion with the author, December 14, 2024.
4. Nathan D. Grawe, *The Agile College: How Institutions Successfully Navigate Demographic Changes* (Johns Hopkins University Press, 2021), 211.
5. John P. Kotter, *Leading Change* (Harvard Business Review Press, 2012), 23.
6. Jennifer Desjarlais (former dean of admission and financial aid, Wellesley College, and principal, Cambridge Hill Partners, Inc.) in discussion with the author, n.d.

7. Frei and Morriss, November 1, 2023.
8. Brené Brown, "Research," https://brenebrown.com/the-research/.
9. Jon Boeckenstedt (vice provost of enrollment management, Oregon State University), email message to author, December 1, 2024.
10. Rajesh Mirchandani (former BBC News correspondent and founder of Storytelling Consulting), in discussion with the author, December 14, 2024.
11. Danny Meyer, "Connect the Dots to Create Exceptional Hospitality Experiences," Global Leadership Network (August 27, 2018), https://globalleadership.org/videos/leading-organizations/connect-the-dots-to-create-exceptional-hospitality-experiences.
12. Coffin, October 31, 2024.
13. Jamil Zaki, "The Strategic Power of Hope," *Harvard Business Review* (December 4, 2024), https://hbr.org/2024/12/the-strategic-power-of-hope.
14. La Jerne Terry Cornish, "Where Do We Go from Here?" (panel discussion, National Association for College Admission Counseling, Los Angeles California, September 28, 2024).
15. Anselment, December 14, 2024.
16. Grawe, *Agile College.*
17. Coffin, October 31, 2024.
18. Simon Sinek, *Start with Why: How Great Leaders Inspire Everyone to Take Action* (Portfolio, 2011), 161.
19. "Vision to Victory: The Art of Storytelling in Leadership," *Maven*, https://maven.com/articles/effective-storytelling-leadership-guide.
20. Mirchandani, December 14, 2024.
21. Desjarlais, n.d.
22. Kasey Urquidez (former vice president, enrollment management, and dean, admissions, University of Arizona), in discussion with the author, February 27, 2024.
23. Mark Steinlage (vice president for enrollment management, Rockhurst University), in discussion with the author, November 7, 2024.
24. Boeckenstedt, December 1, 2024.
25. Whitney Soule (vice provost, dean of admissions, University of Pennsylvania), in discussion with the author, February 13, 2024.

Chapter 4

Epigraph: Adele C. Brumfield (vice president of enrollment management, University of Michigan), in discussion with the author, April 18, 2024.

1. "Shared Governance," Association of Governing Boards, https://agb.org/knowledge-center/board-fundamentals/shared-governance/.
2. "Definition of Shared Governance," Marshall University, https://www.marshall.edu/shared-governance/definition-of-shared-governance/.
3. The 2024 Florida Statutes," Online Sunshine, http://www.leg.state.fl.us/Statutes/index.cfm?App_mode=Display_Statute&Search_String=&URL=1000-1099/1007/Sections/1007.263.html.
4. "Frequently Asked Questions," American University, https://www.american.edu/communityrelations/campus-plan/frequently-asked-questions.cfm; Josh Moody, "California Legislature Bails Out UC Berkeley," *Inside Higher Ed* (March 20, 2022), https://www.insidehighered.com/admissions/article/2022/03/21/california-legislature-ends-uc-berkeleys-enrollment-woes.

5. Johnnie Johnson (vice president for enrollment management, Washington College), in discussion with the author, September 18, 2024.
6. Johnson, September 18, 2024
7. Johnson, September 18, 2024
8. "The 8-Step Process for Leading Change," Kotter International Inc., https://www.kotterinc.com/methodology/8-steps/.
9. Johnson, September 18, 2024.
10. Johnson, September 18, 2024.
11. Johnson, September 18, 2024.
12. Nancy Sanchez, in discussion with the author, n.d.
13. Johnson, September 18, 2024.
14. Johnson, September 18, 2024.
15. Shirley Arakawa, "4 Tips for a Successful Enrollment Leadership Transition," *WittKieffer* (September 19, 2024), https://wittkieffer.com/blog/4-tips-for-a-successful-enrollment-leadership-transition.
16. Johnson, September 18, 2024.
17. Lee Coffin (vice president and dean of admissions and financial aid, Dartmouth College), in discussion with the author, October 31, 2024.
18. Danny Meyer, *Setting the Table: The Transforming Power of Hospitality in Business* (Ecco, 2008), 192.
19. Kasey Urquidez (former vice president, enrollment management, and dean, admissions, University of Arizona), in discussion with the author, February 27, 2024.
20. Adele C. Brumfield (vice provost for enrollment management, University of Michigan), in discussion with the author, April 18, 2024.
21. Brian Rosenberg, *"Whatever It Is, I'm Against It": Resistance to Change in Higher Education* (Harvard Education Press, 2023).
22. Ashley Perzyna (chief operating officer, National Association for College Admission Counseling), in discussion with the author, n.d.
23. Edgar H. Schein, *Humble Inquiry: The Gentle Art of Asking Instead of Telling* (Berrett-Koehler Publishers, 2013), 2.
24. Satyajit Dattagupta (executive vice chancellor, chief enrollment officer, and senior advisor to the president, Northeastern University), in discussion with the author, February 13, 2024.
25. David Brooks, *How to Know a Person: The Art of Seeing Others Deeply and Being Deeply Seen* (Random House, 2023), 115.
26. Brumfield, April 18, 2024.
27. "Ignatian Conversation," Rockhurst University, https://www.rockhurst.edu/about/mission-ministry/ignatian-conversation.
28. Dattagupta, February 13, 2024.
29. Urquidez, February 27, 2024.
30. Ken Anselment (former vice president for enrollment and communication, Lawrence University), in discussion with the author, December 14, 2024.
31. Fumio Sugihara (dean of admissions and financial aid, Hampshire College), in discussion with the author, February 13, 2024.
32. Joseph "J. T." Duck (dean of admissions, Tufts University), in discussion with the author, February 13, 2024.
33. Mark Steinlage (vice president of enrollment management, Rockhurst University), in discussion with the author, November 7, 2024.

34. Jon Boeckenstedt (vice provost of enrollment management, Oregon State University), email message to author, December 1, 2024.
35. Steinlage, November 7, 2024.

Chapter 5

1. Scott Carlson and Lee Gardner, "The Year That Pushed Higher Ed to the Edge," *Chronicle of Higher Education* (December 19, 2020), https://www.chronicle.com/article/the-year-that-pushed-higher-ed-to-the-edge.
2. Kathleen McCartney, "5 Steps New Presidents Should Take," *Inside Higher Ed* (February 2022), https://www.insidehighered.com/advice/2022/02/22/lessons-new-presidents-seasoned-one-opinion.
3. "US Department of Justice Settlement," National Association for College Admission Counseling (NACAC) (October 14, 2022), https://www.nacacnet.org/us-department-of-justice-settlement/.
4. Sanford Pelz, "10 Ways COVID Changed College Admissions," *Buzzwords* (May 2022), https://buzzwords.browning.edu/stories/changes-in-college-admissions.
5. Liam Knox, "FAFSA Fiasco Forces Cuts at Small Colleges," *Inside Higher Ed* (June 28, 2024), https://www.insidehighered.com/news/business/cost-cutting/2024/06/28/fafsa-woes-lead-budget-cuts-small-colleges.
6. Jessica Blake, "American Confidence in Higher Ed Hits Historic Low," *Inside Higher Ed* (July 11, 2023), https://www.insidehighered.com/news/business/financial-health/2023/07/11/american-confidence-higher-ed-hits-historic-low; Mary Ellen Flannery, "Anti—DEI Laws Take Aim at Students of Color and LGBTQ+ Students," *NeaToday* (February 14, 2024), https://www.nea.org/nea-today/all-news-articles/anti-dei-laws-take-aim-students-color-and-lgbtq-students; Sara Weissman, "Looking Back and Looking Ahead," *Inside Higher Ed* (April 19, 2023), https://www.insidehighered.com/news/admissions/traditional-age/2023/04/19/looking-back-and-looking-ahead; Kamaron McNair, "Campus Protests, FAFSA Delays Plagued College Admissions This Year—How It Affects Incoming Students, from College Counselors," *CNBC* (May 8, 2024), https://www.cnbc.com/2024/05/08/campus-protests-fafsa-delays-plague-college-admissions-process.htm.
7. Neal Riley, "Emerson College Says Enrollment Down Significantly After 'Negative' Reaction to Student Protests; Layoffs Planned," *CBS News* (June 19, 2024), https://www.cbsnews.com/boston/news/emerson-college-enrollment-protests-layoffs/.
8. Robert Iger, *The Ride of a Lifetime: Lessons Learned from 15 Years as CEO of the Walt Disney Company* (Random House, 2019), 229.
9. Fumio Sugihara (dean of admissions and financial aid, Hampshire College), in discussion with the author, February 13, 2024.
10. Britt Andreatta, *Wired to Resist: The Brain Science of Why Change Fails and a New Model for Driving Success* (7th Mind Publishing, 2017), 46.
11. Erika H. James and Lynn Perry Wooten, *The Prepared Leader: Emerge from Any Crisis More Resilient Than Before* (Wharton School Press, 2022), 63.
12. Erik Larson, "Infographic: Diversity + Inclusion = Better Decision Making at Work," *Cloverpop* (September 19, 2017), https://www.cloverpop.com/blog/infographic-diversity-inclusion-better-decision-making-at-work.
13. James and Wooten, *Prepared Leader*, 54.
14. Tahira Crawford (senior associate director, director of multicultural recruitment, Columbia University), in discussion with the author, n.d.

15. Satyajit Dattagupta (Executive vice chancellor, chief enrollment officer, and senior advisor to the president , Northeastern University), in discussion with the author, February 13, 2024.
16. Adele C. Brumfield (vice provost for enrollment management, University of Michigan), in discussion with the author, April 18, 2024.
17. Dale Elwood, cited in McCartney, "5 Steps."
18. Chrissy Scivicque, "How to Master the Necessary Skill of Professional Detachment," *Eat Your Career* (July 11, 2022), https://eatyourcareer.com/2022/07/how-to-master-the-necessary-skill-of-professional-detachment/.
19. Joseph Montgomery (associate vice provost for enrollment management, North Carolina Agriculture and Technical State College), in discussion with the author, September 13, 2024.
20. Whitney Soule (vice provost and dean of admissions, University of Pennsylvania), in discussion with the author, February 13, 2024.
21. Soule, February 13, 2024.
22. Ryan Holiday, posted November 12, 2024, "Using Ancient Wisdom to Solve Modern Problems," *Masterclass* video, chapter 1, 13:32:00, https://www.masterclass.com/series/using-ancient-wisdom-to-solve-modern-problems.
23. Joseph "J. T." Duck (dean of admissions, Tufts University), in discussion with the author, February 13, 2024.
24. James and Wooten, *Prepared Leader*, 45.
25. James and Wooten, *Prepared Leader*, 29–30.
26. Nicholas Janni, *Leader as Healer: A New Paradigm for 21st-Century Leadership* (LID Publishing, 2022), 78.
27. Kasey Urquidez (former vice president, enrollment management, and dean, admissions, University of Arizona), in discussion with the author, February 27, 2024.
28. Ken Anselment (former vice president for enrollment and communication, Lawrence University), in discussion with the author, December 14, 2024.
29. Duck, February 13, 2024.
30. Soule, February 13, 2024.
31. Mark Steinlage (vice president of enrollment management, Rockhurst University), in discussion with the author, November 7, 2024.
32. Dattagupta, February 13, 2024.
33. Steinlage, November 7, 2024.
34. Jon Boeckenstedt (vice provost of enrollment management, Oregon State University), email to the author, December 1, 2024.

Chapter 6

Epigraph: Bill George and Peter Sims, *True North* (Jossey Bass, 2007), 36.

1. Angel B. Perez, "One CEO's Story of Executive Burnout," The Association for Education Leadership (ASAE), February 7, 2023, https://www.asaecenter.org/resources/articles/an_plus/2023/2-february/one-ceos-story-of-executive-burnout.
2. Ethan Sawyer, interview with Angel B. Perez, College Essay Guy, podcast interview, "401: NACAC CEO Angel Pérez—Self-Care for Counselors, Leaders, and Professionals in Helping Roles," July 20, 2023, https://www.collegeessayguy.com/podcast-stream/self-care-for-professionals-in-helping-roles.
3. David Chang, *Eat a Peach: A Memoir* (Clarkson Potter, 2020), 52.

4. "How Stress Impacts Decision Making," Walden University, https://www.waldenu.edu/online-masters-programs/ms-in-clinical-mental-health-counseling/resource/how-stress-impacts-decision-making.
5. "What Oprah Knows for Sure About Saying 'No,'" Oprah.com, https://www.oprah.com/omagazine/what-oprah-knows-for-sure-about-always-saying-yes.
6. "Designing Your Life," https://designingyour.life/.
7. Bill Burnett and Dave Evans, *Designing Your Life: How to Build a Well-Lived Joyful Life* (Alfred A. Knopf, 2016), 50–54.
8. Greg McKeown, *Essentialism: The Disciplined Pursuit of Less* (Crown Currency, 2014), 109.
9. Steve Jobs, "Focus Is about Saying No"—Steve Jobs, Worldwide Developers Conference 97, Lecture, San Jose, California, May 19997, video of lecture, 00.01, https://www.youtube.com/watch?v=0GD57UQg4X4.
10. Ryan Holiday, *Stillness Is the Key* (Portfolio, 2019), 201.
11. Robin Sharma, *The Energy Explosion* (Sharma Leadership International, Inc., 2006), audiobook, 0:06:00, accessed via Audible, https://www.audible.com/pd/The-Energy-Explosion-Audiobook/B002V8MY26?qid=1734019016&sr=1–1&ref_pageloadid=not_applicable&pf_rd_p=83218cca-c308-412f-bfcf-90198b687a2f&pf_rd_r=0MCHBAB4SCREQFFF9AR6&plink=FqTtLW8HzDtbNx0x&pageLoadId=BkAjzw3cz4GzOvcE&creativeId=0d6f6720-f41c-457e-a42b-8c8dceb62f2c&ref=a_search_c3_lProduct_1_1.
12. Cathryn Lavery, "Why Creating a Meaningful Morning Routine Will Make You More Successful," *Mission.org*, January 24, 2019, https://medium.com/the-mission/how-creating-a-meaningful-morning-routine-will-make-you-more-successful-1b7372655938.
13. "The Mental Health Benefits of Exercise—HelpGuide.Org," November 2, 2018, https://www.helpguide.org/wellness/fitness/the-mental-health-benefits-of-exercise.
14. Holiday, *Stillness Is the Key*, 215.
15. Timothy J. Legg, Jon Johnson, "Negative Effects of Technology: Psychological, Social, and Health," *Medical News Today*, February 25, 2020, https://www.medicalnewstoday.com/articles/negative-effects-of-technology.
16. "Robin Sharma, *The Wealth Money Can't Buy: The 8 Hidden Habits to Live Your Richest Life* (Crown Currency, 2024), 361.
17. Holiday, *Stillness Is the Key*, 215.
18. Robert L. Smith, *A Quaker Book of Wisdom: Life Lessons in Simplicity, Service, and Common Sense* (William and Morrow Company, Inc, 1998), 3.
19. Arthur C. Brooks, "Why You Should Want to Be Alone," *The Atlantic* (July 11, 2024), https://www.theatlantic.com/ideas/archive/2024/07/hermit-solitude-benefits-happiness/678955/.
20. Thuy-vy T. Nguyen, Richard M. Ryan, and Edward L. Deci, "Solitude as an Approach to Affective Self-Regulation," *Personality and Social Psychology Bulletin* 44, no. 1 (January 1, 2018): 92–106, https://doi.org/10.1177/0146167217733073.
21. Frank Ostaseski and Rachel Naomi Remen, *The Five Invitations: Discovering What Death Can Teach Us About Living Fully* (Flatiron Books, 2019), 182.
22. Diana Chapman Walsh, *The Claims of Life: A Memoir* (The MIT Press, 2023), 123.
23. Cal Newport, *Slow Productivity: The Lost Art of Accomplishment Without Burnout* (Portfolio, 2024), 136–142.
24. Ashley Perzyna (chief operating officer, National Association for College Admission Counseling), in discussion with the author, n.d.
25. Ken Anselment (former vice president for enrollment and communication, Lawrence University), in discussion with the author, December 14, 2024.

26. Kasey Urquidez (former vice president, enrollment management, and dean, admissions, University of Arizona), in discussion with the author, February 27, 2024.
27. Fumio Sugihara (dean of admission and financial aid, Hampshire College), in discussion with the author, February 13, 2024.
28. Whitney Soule (vice provost and dean of admissions, University of Pennsylvania), in discussion with the author, February 13, 2024.
29. Urquidez, February 27, 2024.
30. Joseph "J. T." Duck (dean of admissions, Tufts University), in discussion with the author, February 13, 2024.
31. Mark Steinlage (vice president of enrollment management, Rockhurst University), in discussion with the author, November 7, 2024.
32. Johnnie Johnson, vice president of enrollment management, Washington College.
33. Steinlage, November 7, 2024.

Conclusion

Epigraph: Simon Sinek, Start with Why: *How Great Leaders Inspire Everyone to Take Action* (Portfolio, 2011), blurb.

1. "The Toughest Job You'll Ever Love: What Peace Corps Gave Me," Peace Corps, https://www.peacecorps.gov/costa-rica/stories/toughest-job-youll-ever-love-what-peace-corps-gave-me/.
2. Satyajit Dattagupta (executive vice chancellor, chief enrollment officer, and senior advisor to the president, Northeastern University), in discussion with the author, February 13, 2024.
3. Anoop Dhiman, "The Obstacle in the Path Becomes the Path," *Medium* (June 9, 2023), https://medium.com/@anoopdhiman/the-obstacle-in-the-path-becomes-the-path-d9de79924775.
4. Solcyré Burga, "What Trump's Win Means for Education," *TIME* (November 8, 2024), https://time.com/7174651/what-trump-winning-means-for-education/.
5. Liam Knox, Jessica Blake, and Katherine Knott, "Education Department Lays Off Nearly Half of Staff," *Inside Higher Ed* (March 11, 2025), https://www.insidehighered.com/news/government/politics-elections/2025/03/11/education-department-reduce-staff-half; U.S. Department of Education, "Title VI of the Civil Rights Act in Light of Students for Fair Admissions v. Harvard," letter to educational institutions, February 14, 2025, https://www.ed.gov/media/document/dear-colleague-letter-sffa-v-harvard-109506.pdf.
6. Michael D. Watkins, *The First 90 Days: Proven Strategies for Getting Up to Speed Faster and Smarter, Updated and Expanded* (Harvard Business Review Press, 2013).
7. Bill Burnett and Dave Evans, *Designing Your Life: How to Build a Well-Lived, Joyful Life* (Alfred A. Knopf, 2016).
8. John P. Kotter, *Leading Change* (Harvard Review Business Press, 2012).
9. Danny Meyer, *The Transforming Power of Hospitality in Business* (Ecco Press, 2008).
10. Cal Newport, *Slow Productivity: The Lost Art of Accomplishment Without Burnout* (Portfolio, 2024).
11. Ryan Holiday, *Stillness is the Key* (Portfolio, 2019).
12. Edgar H. Schein and Peter A. Schein, *Humble Inquiry: The Gentle Art of Asking Instead of Telling* (Berrett-Koehler Publishers, 2013).

Acknowledgments

I stand on the shoulders of giants. I am fortunate to have "grown up" in the profession with mentors, advisors, and coaches who took me under their wing, bosses who took a chance on me, and colleagues who saw leadership potential in me before I could ever see it in myself. Gracias Joyce Hansen, Michael Mehmet, Sheryl Olivers, Irma Lederer, Mary Lou Bates, John Young, Roz Estrada, Dean Joseph Tolliver, Sue Layden, Dr. Peggy Boyle, Sean Callaway, Mitchell Thompson, Carla Shere, Beryl Jeffers, Richard Alvarez, Lisa Sohmer, Carl "Sandy" Behrend, Victoria Romero, Dick Vos, Thyra Briggs, Dr. Arnaldo Rodriguez, Pat Coleman, Dr. Esther Hugo, Dr. Laura Trombley, Robin Mamlet, Dr. Scott Thomas, Dr. Linda Perkins, Dr. Daryl Smith, Dr. Joanne Berger-Sweeney, Lee Coffin, Justin Draeger, Sue Cunningham, Ian O'Loughlin, Dr. Barry Glassner, and Jennifer Desjarlais.

Writing a book requires a leap of faith, not just on my part, but on the part of many people who believed this book was an important contribution to higher education. The team at Harvard Education Press is the most enthusiastic in the business, and I couldn't be more grateful for their support. Gracias Jayne Fargnoli, former editor-in-chief of Harvard Education Press, who strongly encouraged me to write this book and was patient in accommodating my hectic schedule. Her excitement for the content of the book inspired me to complete the project. I have SO much gratitude for my editor, Molly Cerrone, whose wise counsel made the book stronger and whose precision with grammar and language arts is awe inspiring. I'm also grateful to Alexis Redding at the Harvard Graduate School of Education, whose encouragement, support, and counsel took me from book concept to final manuscript. And, of course, I have the utmost gratitude for my research assistant, Cameron Hair. Her extraordinary attention to detail, willingness to question every one of my claims, and passion for the field of education research are why she was the perfect partner on this project.

I send heartfelt gratitude to each of the deans who took time out of their hectic schedules to interview for this book, send notes via email, or have side conversations at conferences that helped make this book stronger. Your advice continues to inspire me, and I know it will inspire the admission professionals who will read this book. I'm also grateful to Jennifer Desjarlais and Ken Anselment, two giants in our field whom I admire greatly, who read the book in advance and gave me suggestions for making it stronger. I still pinch myself that Jennifer agreed to write the foreword to this book.

Finally, I'm grateful to the NACAC board and staff members (past and present), whom I have the honor of partnering with on this incredible journey. I learn so much from them, and their commitment to the organization's mission and vision energizes me each day. The organization (and profession) is replete with passionate people trying to make a difference in the world, and I count my lucky stars each day that I get to be a part of it.

Onward!

About the Author

Angel B. Pérez, PhD, is CEO of the National Association for College Admission Counseling (NACAC). He represents more than twenty-eight thousand admission and counseling professionals worldwide committed to postsecondary access and success. Pérez is recognized as a national thought leader and sought-after speaker on issues of educational equity, access, and success. Prior to joining NACAC, Dr. Pérez served in higher education leadership positions, most recently, as vice president for enrollment and student success at Trinity College in Connecticut. During his time in Connecticut, the governor appointed him to the New England Board of Higher Education, and he served on Forward50, a group of higher education leaders presenting solutions to Congress. He is a contributor and frequent commentator in media outlets, including *The New York Times, Washington Post, The Hill, NPR, Forbes, PBS NewsHour, The Atlantic*, and *CBS Evening News*. Dr. Pérez's passion for teaching led him to serve as a faculty member at Trinity College's Educational Studies Department, UCLA's College Counseling Certification Program, and the Harvard Graduate School of Education. He also served as a visiting international faculty member at Rikkyo University in Japan. His trusteeships include the Berkshire School, United World College in Costa Rica, Hartford Youth Scholars, Tuition Exchange, Scholarship America, and the Council for the Advancement and Support of Education. He is a member of the Wall Street Journal CEO Council.

Index